To Al + Shiz Hikida
With Aloha +
Best Wishes from
Hawaii

Best Wishes
George Ariyoshi

WITH
OBLIGATION
TO ALL

WITH
OBLIGATION
TO ALL

George R. Ariyoshi

ARIYOSHI FOUNDATION
HONOLULU

Printed in the United States of America

01 00 99 98 97 96 5 4 3 2 1

Distributed by
University of Hawai'i Press
2840 Kolowalu Street
Honolulu, HI 96822
(808) 956-8255

Library of Congress Cataloguing-in-Publication Data

Ariyoshi, George R., 1926-
With obligation to all / George R. Ariyoshi.
p.   cm.
Includes index.
ISBN 0-8248-1941-1
1. Ariyoshi, George R., 1926-   —Biography.
2. Governors—Hawaii—Biography.
3. Hawaii—Politics and government—1900-1959.
4. Hawaii—Politics and government—1959-
I. Title.
DU627.83.A75A3   1997   996.9'04'092—dc21   96-39505

This book is printed on acid-free paper
and meets the guidelines for permanence and durability
of the Council on Library Resources.

CONTENTS

Dedicated to my father and mother,
Ryozo and Mitsue Ariyoshi,
whose sacrifice made everything else possible;
to my wife Jean,
who is the constant light of my life;
to my children, Lynn, Ryozo, and Donn,
who so immediately motivated me;
and to my grandson Sky,
who represents the future.

ACKNOWLEDGEMENTS

NOTHING QUITE MOVED ME TO THE WORK of this book as the birth of our grandson, Sky. My wife Jean reviewed the text several times and helped order the photo sections. After the first extensive draft, I elicited helpful comments and suggestions from George Akita, professor emeritus of history, University of Hawaii at Manoa; Dr. Akira Iriye, professor of American history at Harvard University; Kent Keith, former director of the Department of Planning and Economic Development (more recently president of Chaminade University); Dr. Akemi Kikumura, curator of the Japanese American National Museum in Los Angeles; Hideto Kono, my first director of the Department of Planning and Economic Development (more recently president of the Japan-America Institute of Management Science); Dr. Richard Kosaki, former chancellor, University of Hawaii (more recently president of Tokai University); Mildred Kosaki, researcher and writer; Dr. Margaret Oda, former Honolulu district superintendent of the Department of Education; Dr. Dennis Ogawa, professor of American studies, University of Hawaii; and Susumu Ono, former administrative director and also chairman of the State Department of Land and Natural Resources.

Many others reviewed specific passages or supplied pieces of information—more than I can adequately acknowledge.

INTRODUCTION

BY THE TIME GOVERNOR ARIYOSHI INVITED ME to come by his office, I found myself anticipating the voice which speaks softly. I had interviewed him in 1992 and 1993 on historical subjects, and he obviously had a great deal on his mind. When I appeared for my appointment in late 1993, he talked about having become a grandfather. A part of him was far away, in conversation with his young grandson in some future time. He expressed a deep sense of the passing of an era, but that was all the more reason to generate ideas and answers for the future. He had not come to rest on his numerous laurels. He worried about the declining quality of public life in the State and around the country. He wanted to keep moving and do his part.

While I had not been personally close to him, he seemed to appreciate the fact that I had maintained an interest in the relationship between past and present in Hawaii. He said he was thinking of writing a book. He asked if I would serve as an editor and writer, but above all as a questioner who helped him turn through pages of the past.

I thought of when I first saw him during the 1968 Legislature, the first year in the then-new State Capitol. It was a legislative session that was considerably less elegant than the building itself. A factional conflict raged within the Democratic Party, and I most vividly remember Ariyoshi during a recess in the floor action. While various senators huddled and murmured, Ariyoshi took a chair near the back of the chamber, by the clock, alone, a faction of one.

I learned that in the pre-session caucuses of the 1967-1968 Legislature, he had declined to trade his vote to either of the two contending sides. There was a rumor that he had been offered the Senate presidency, but mysteriously he had declined. When the positions of power were finally distributed, he was left with next to nothing.

As a political reporter, I was to see other politicians shut out of power by organizational battles. They tended to plod along, and then, when the pressure level rose, erupt in anger. Ariyoshi seemed unphased. He was self-contained and unfailingly gracious.

I remember dropping by his office a couple of times out of curiosity, but there seemed to be little to talk about. He had the great smile and bearing that are so useful to a candidate, but he peered out at the world from some detached, abstract place that was not to be quickly fathomed. I had to check the election records to learn how successful he had been at the polls, because he was not what you may think of as a politician. He seemed reserved almost to the point of shyness. He did not crave the limelight. He was oblivious to publicity. I could as well have been a delivery boy or a bank president—the courtesies, I sensed, would have been the same. It was beyond imagining that within two years he would be elected lieutenant governor and play such a major role in the hotly contested reelection of the legendary incumbent, John A. Burns. That he would then become governor a longer time even than John Burns, and longer than anyone ever will be again under the revised State Constitution, was not to be guessed at. So while I may have dropped by that year, I essentially failed to understand much about his inner reserves, or about his potential.

Would I now, in 1993, like to sit with him and ask him questions? I quickly agreed. I wanted to know if it was true that he had been offered the presidency of the Senate. How exactly had he come to run with Governor Burns in 1970? What lay behind his insistence on referring to Japanese values? What sustained this gentle, soft-spoken person in the harsh world of politics?

It occurred to me that, collectively, we in Hawaii seem so certain we know about the 1950s and 1960s, but we are so uncertain about more recent times. We know about the Democratic Revolution of 1954 and Statehood in 1959 (and many people in Hawaii make claims on the legend of John Burns), but the 1970s and 1980s seem to mystify us. No one was in a better position to shed light on that period than Ariyoshi.

Typically he and I would be scheduled to work an hour and a half, but we would work three hours or more. We taped, reviewed transcripts, made endless notes, leaned in this or that direction, regrouped, and pushed on. In the process I discovered an inner intensity, which he revealed in slow, subtle progressions. Imagine an inherent modesty, an absence of theatrics, and an absence of egotism, but nonetheless a fire is burning.

There is the well-known story that as a child he overcame a speech defect. As with his defect of speech, as with shyness, as with running for office, I think he had to struggle initially with the writing of a book. He quickly roughed out his philosophy of government and the vignettes that illuminated it. But tone and texture emerged slowly; the more personal perspective emerged slowly.

I should underscore that well before the gubernatorial election of

1994, he had spelled out most of what he had to say about the principles of government. The point is that his original statements were not intended as a critique of the present State administration, although inevitably some now may be interpreted as such. His approach was typically philosophical, and other than a few persons, such as Burns, he did not speak about personalities at all. With prompting, what little he had to say about his rivals was usually kind to the point where it could have been said comfortably in their presence.

As part of our process, I had the opportunity to talk with his close acquaintances—from his wry and insightful boyhood friend George Akita (the "other GA"), now a scholar of Japanese history; to Sus Ono, a self-effacing and infinitely knowledgeable Mandarin of government; to Kent Keith, who spent endless hours with Ariyoshi generating new ideas during Ariyoshi's last term as governor, even though Ariyoshi by then was in his tenth year in office. Familiarity can indeed breed contempt, but people who have worked closely with Ariyoshi like him immensely—like him and often revere him. While this is a simple observation, it is worth making, because so many people in politics today look better in the eye of the camera than in the eye of the beholder.

The resulting text of *With Obligation to All* does not attempt to be a comprehensive memoir. It does not attempt to address the entire record, or have the last word. Rather, it attempts to reveal the political story of contemporary Hawaii in terms which may be useful in the future. My job was to help make the story accessible, and not to comment, but I would like to make a brief introductory comment here on the historical context of Governor Ariyoshi's story.

First, Ariyoshi's election as the first governor of Japanese ancestry completed the agenda of transformation which occurred during the 1950s and 1960s in the racial, social, and political climate of Hawaii. We have to pinch ourselves today to recall the prejudice aimed at people of Japanese ancestry, but if you read Lawrence Fuchs' *Hawaii Pono,* or Gary Okihiro's *Cane Fires,* the story is still there. Unique among all groups, people of Japanese ancestry were incessantly nagged, questioned, criticized and accused falsely. It is embarrassing to hark up and repeat things which were said, but in the Archives of Hawaii, you can trace a line of attack and innuendo which runs all the way from Annexation to Statehood to the time of Ariyoshi's election. It can be crudely paraphrased as, "Be careful, or the Japanese will take over." It was whispered by the Annexationists to Washington, constantly repeated by the sugar planters, and then taken up by a generation of people in the 1920s and

1930s who wrote wildly untrue military intelligence reports about the loyalties of AJAs in the event of war with Japan. Pre-war visiting writers routinely spun long passages about Hawaii's "Japanese problem," an insidious code which one was not to question, the lie which said it all.

Ariyoshi himself seems to have been touched minimally by prejudice, but what the *nisei* veterans of World War II addressed on the battlefield, he was left to finish off as the first governor of Japanese ancestry in Hawaii, and the first governor of color in America. He helped define not only who sat in the Legislature and Congress, but who exercised power in high executive office. That his long administration was a model of fairness and openness was therefore not only of short-term political significance, but long-term social significance. That his obsession with equality of opportunity went all but unnoticed is a mark of his quietly living up to this ideal year after year, for the thirteen years he served as governor.

His election had no sooner completed one agenda of change than a whole new agenda was forced upon him. I think we now can see more clearly that Ariyoshi came into high office in Hawaii when American liberalism, as it had been defined, was coming unravelled. The era of Kennedy and Johnson was giving way to the era of Nixon and Reagan. Ariyoshi responded by being himself. He looked to himself, his heritage, and to Hawaii. He carried forward the Democratic era in Hawaii in the face of the national Republican tide. He generated new thinking which was beyond partisanship, and which so thoroughly reflected the uniqueness of Hawaii.

After Hawaii's long pursuit of Statehood, after Hawaii had reveled in all things imagined to be American, Ariyoshi was able to see and sense the Hawaii that is separate and different. After a period in which all things of Japanese origin had been suppressed and denied, Ariyoshi had the courage to draw on his Japanese heritage for inspiration and guidance.

In the process he made a unique contribution to the political culture of Hawaii and America—a contribution which I have come to see as a deep and special sense of balance and interrelatedness. It is distinguished by a deep concern not only for the individual but the community, by an intense passion not only for the political moment but for the distant tomorrow.

Tom Coffman

WITH
OBLIGATION
TO ALL

CHAPTER ONE

Otagai

On a beautiful Hawaiian day in December, 1974, my wife Jean and I, along with the Chief Justice of Hawaii and several others, were seated in the gazebo at Iolani Palace, waiting. The ornate, circular gazebo stands on a raised platform which looks out in all directions. It was built for the coronation of David Kalakaua, the last king of Hawaii. It also was used for the coronation of his sister, Liliʻuokalani, the last reigning Hawaiian monarch. As you face the audience from the vantage point of the gazebo, the modern towers of downtown Honolulu rise behind you. Iolani Palace looms above you to the left. It is the only royal palace in America and a symbol of the independent nation which existed before the overthrow of the Kingdom of Hawaii. Beyond the Palace, further toward the mountains, rises the much larger form of the State Capitol. Its rich synthesis of Polynesian, Western, and Asian design themes was inspired by the intense enthusiasm that was generated by the achievement of Statehood.

Iolani Palace and the capitol together help tell the unique story of a one-time nation which is now—geographically, politically, and historically—the most unusual state of the United States.

I had begun my public service here in 1954, as the most junior member of the Territorial Legislature, when the Democratic Party swept away a half-century of rule by the Republican Party. I was part of a broadly based social and political movement, one of many people working in a shared cause. Accordingly, I saw inauguration day as the culmination of the work and sacrifice of many people.

It was a last step in creating a new public ethic of equal opportunity, displacing the old system of special privilege. For non-white people, both in Hawaii and America, it was the beginning of executive responsibility at the statehouse level. In this sense, inauguration day provided a nice, clearcut breakthrough. It was a step along the path of great social changes that had occurred in the post-war era.

Less clearly, 1974 harked up perplexing new challenges. I was a visible symbol of change, but the exhilaration of the early years of Statehood for Hawaii had substantially run its course. Nationally, the Democratic coalition was weakening. The Democratic Party in Hawaii—despite its repeated victories—was strained by new excesses of factionalism.

What lay ahead of me was more than a task of renewal. It was a task of redefining where we were going. Ultimately this new political direction would have to do with combining a liberal sense of community and a conservative approach to the management of resources, including government finances. As I write, this new direction is still lacking an adequate vocabulary, both in Hawaii and around the country. But with each year I believe more firmly that our actions during the 1970s in Hawaii offered clear guides to the direction we should be taking now, and the direction we must take in the future.

The base that I had been given for my job was derived from the passionate liberalism of the postwar Democratic Party and the strong value system—in many ways an inherently conservative value system—of my Japanese immigrant parents. I had grown up hearing an incessant message of obligation. To fulfill this idea of obligation was to be involved with the entire spectrum of the community, to make commitments, and to take risks in service to the long view of history. From the gazebo, in the front row of the large crowd, I could see the smiling faces of my mother, Mitsue, and our family's three children, Lynn, Ryozo, and Donn. Nothing so motivated me as the interconnection that they suggested—the challenge of relating the past to the future, the challenge of not only understanding where we had been, but envisioning where we should be going.

As I looked around, I could see my designated cabinet and many close associates. Some had supported me in every one of my election campaigns over twenty years. I saw long-time allies from the Democratic Party, as well as some adversaries. All were people whose cooperation I would need. The same was true of the Republicans. If their party was identified with a discredited, bygone time, they had turned out to be likable and often admirable as individuals.

I thought how much I would have liked to see my father, Ryozo Ariyoshi. I was comforted by the fact that he had passed away believing the day would come when I would be sworn in as governor. I also longed for the presence of the man I succeeded in office, John A. Burns. He had challenged me to become active in public life, and he had guided me into the governorship. Governor Burns watched the proceedings from his hospital bed.

I believed the first Democratic election victory in 1954 had dramatically uplifted the great majority of people in Hawaii, but I also had learned that getting power was one thing and using it well was another. I wanted to make further advances in the process of social and economic change. I also had to respond to new challenges, but the question is always how. It is easy to talk about change, but how do you take risks and actually bring about needed change?

I had left most of the planning for the Inauguration to supporters while I concentrated on organizing my cabinet and staff. A search committee generated names and leads. I made a point of telling the committee that I didn't care whether the prospective cabinet members had supported me politically. I didn't care whether they had supported my opponents. I cared about their character and ability. I went over and over the names until I settled on virtually everyone I wanted on the entire team. I wanted people who thought, "What a great opportunity to do something!" I decided that if individuals had to dwell on the decision for more than a few days, it might reflect some deeply held reservation. After I decided on virtually every position, I began talking to potential team members on a Wednesday. Most people gave me a yes on the spot. To the few who couldn't make the commitment immediately I said, "You have until Monday." By the close of day Monday, I had my team.

Not only the quality of the people, but the process of how you bring them together, is important. You must capitalize on the fact that when people embark on a great venture, they're excited and have great hopes. A team needs to share in positive feelings, which means they need to come together and be part of the Inauguration, when spirits are high.

I myself felt a tremendous excitement, but I was awed by the responsibility. As a result of Hawaii's unique history, as well as its separation from the rest of the United States, the State Constitution prescribes the most centralized state government in the union. As I stood to recite my oath of office, my vow to support and defend the constitutions of the State of Hawaii and the United States of America was destined to be of more than ritual significance. In my attention to the uniqueness of Hawaii, I was to get into serious conflict with the U.S. Constitution several times, but such a possibility never occurred to me as I set out.

In my address, I talked about what I then could see of a new direction. Today I feel good about that address because it reflected a conviction that Hawaii is an extraordinary, different, and special place, and that we have a special responsibility for its care. This feeling of Hawaii's uniqueness was only to become stronger in the years ahead. I talked about controlling economic development in keeping with "our unique insular nature." I talked about the pursuit of self-sufficiency in food and

energy, and about guiding the growth and distribution of our population. Above all I talked about stewardship. We could not merely take
from the community. We had to *take care of* the community and its
resources. We had an obligation to build on what had gone before us.
We had to not only meet the needs of the present, but pass on the opportunity of a good life to future generations. Just as Jack Burns had
pledged change twelve years earlier in this same setting, I too pledged
change, "not just for the sake of change, but change to meet new needs
and new times."

Governor Burns was a larger-than-life figure. My job was not merely
to carry on but to carry his legacy into uncharted places. I had never
dwelled on the idea of being the first governor in America of Japanese
ancestry, or the first American governor of non-white ancestry. But
breaking that barrier was central to Jack Burns' thinking. Inevitably that
barrier had been on the minds of some of the people who had supported
me, and it had become my job to break down the barrier. Now, in the
terms of my Japanese ancestry, it was my obligation to avoid bringing
shame, *haji*. But for people of today to understand such a seemingly
ancient idea, it is necessary to begin at the beginning.

MY FATHER WAS LEAN AND MUSCULAR, and he was known in his
younger days for his skill as a *sumo* wrestler. When I was a boy I always
saw him as strong and self-assured. He guided me with a sense of confidence and certainty. When I grew up I was amazed to learn how difficult
his life had been. He was born in a small village in the prefecture of
Fukuoka, Japan. Although he was an excellent student, he only went to
school through the third grade. When he was young he went to sea.
When he arrived in Hawaii he liked what he saw and jumped ship. As a
result, he struggled not only with being an immigrant who spoke little
English, but also with being an illegal alien. During World War II, he
lived with the expectation that he would be interned.

In the ancient sport of *sumo*, wrestlers are given special names. His
sumo name was "Yahata Yama," and for many years he was known casu-
ally by this name, and not Ariyoshi. The first year I was to campaign,
which was thirty-five years after his arrival in Hawaii, I was surprised to
hear people greet him as "Yahata."

We moved a lot, but I remember best our two-room place at the corner of Smith and Pauahi streets in Chinatown, just above Honolulu harbor. One of those rooms was a dining room, living room, and a bedroom
as well. In Japanese style the dining table was low and we sat on mats on

the floor while we ate. At bedtime, the table was rolled away and our *futon* bedding was unrolled onto the mat floor.

Papa often worked on the waterfront as a stevedore. He also got work as a stone mason, but he had an entrepreneurial streak. He contracted to supply gravel to road builders, and he quarried the rock, which required the blasting of dynamite. He didn't want to ask anybody else to do it, so he learned to blast the dynamite himself. He also made *tofu* and sold it, and he eventually opened a dry-cleaning shop in lower Kalihi. He was also to become a campaigner with seemingly boundless reserves of energy.

My mother was from Kumamoto Prefecture, which is next to Fukuoka in southwestern Japan. Like my father she had only an elementary-school education. Also like my father, she had an amazing way of seeing the bright side of things when she might have despaired. Because our family shared a communal kitchen, she usually got up at four-thirty to start the day's cooking. When she cooked our favorite dishes, she would announce she wasn't hungry. In fact she said she did not care for a particular dish, and she would pass her share on to us. At the time I thought it strange that she did not care for such delicious food, and it was not until long afterward that I saw through her little story.

My parents' idea of opportunity was the opportunity to work hard, be free to improve their lot in life, and raise a family. I was born in 1926, the first of six children. I had one brother and four sisters. Although our two rooms were on the second floor of a rough-board building, I never thought of our place as a tenement, nor did I think of ourselves as poor.

We had a positive sense of our neighborhood, our schools, and of Hawaii itself. Family life sheltered us, and within this nurturing environment we practiced discipline willingly and happily. We were free to venture out, but I adhered to the boundaries set by my parents. My mother wanted to know what I was doing, so I always told her, "*Okaasan,* I'm going to such-and-such a place." If I was going to some other place afterward, I would go back and tell her where I would be next, so she always knew where I was. From that point of view, I was quite protected. We were a tightly knit family, and my parents were totally in control, yet I didn't feel I was being deprived of freedom.

I was constantly told there was a right path, and there was no question that I was to follow it. My father was always saying to me, "Do the things that are right. Never mind what happens." I should add that he often told me, "Be number one. Be the best."

His beliefs were derived from a code that was both an inner code and a community code. The two ran together so harmoniously as to be almost one and the same. What you knew to be right came from within, yet it was intertwined with the individual doing right in the eyes of others. He used the Japanese word *otagai,* referring to the deep Japanese sense of mutual obligation. He used the words *okage sama de,* an expression of appreciation for the support and assistance of others, which is sometimes translated as, "I am what I am because of you."

He would say, "Remember to be considerate of other people. Be grateful that you can get help from other people. Acknowledge others. Be humble, because many other people help make things possible for you."

The essence of my father's thinking accompanied me through my career and into the governorship. In my role as governor, I began using some of the Japanese words my father had used to explain my beliefs. *Okage sama de,* because of your shadow which falls on me, because of your help, because of you, I am what I am. I reminded myself of that idea often, and I tried to nurture that attitude in others. We are extensions of one another, and we are beholden to one another.

A little background on the use of the Japanese language is in order. Up to the time I became governor, Japanese was only used informally, or as slang, in the political life of Hawaii. If someone told you, with a shrug of the shoulders, *shikata ga nai,* you were being told, "Such-and-such can't be helped." In pidgin English it was, "No can help." But Japanese words and phrases were not used as a way of discussing values and concepts. On the contrary, persons of Japanese ancestry had been placed under great pressure during World War II to suppress all that was Japanese about themselves. Our first-generation people were sent to English classes in what was called the "Speak American" campaign. The loyalty of many people was questioned, and some reacted understandably, by turning away from all public reference to our Japanese past. Every aspect of our lives was put to the test, "Is it American?"

By the time I gained some political awareness, I had come to feel strongly that everyone should be encouraged to be themselves. *Okage sama de* and other such statements reflected values that my father and his generation had given to us as a new generation of Americans. In my role as the first governor of Japanese and non-white ancestry, I felt it was my duty to speak candidly about my roots, and to be accepting of myself, in order to encourage others to be accepting of themselves.

I came to see that each of us is limited until we are ready to acknowledge that we may be different. Each of us is unique. Each of us has his or her own background. To be what and who we really are is the best way to contribute as Americans. To succeed in being ourselves, we must be treated equally in spite of our differences. As a result of being treated equally, every person can be made to feel comfortable. By practicing equality, people will feel good about themselves and good about others.

The development of equality, the practice of equality, the infusion of confidence that gives a daily reality to the concept of equality—these have been among our most important achievements in Hawaii over the past half century. From our past we should distill and celebrate this fundamental point. In this process, elective politics has played a central role. Our sense of community, of being connected to one another, is likewise an important part of our heritage.

As an officeholder I tried to remain keenly aware that I was an extension of the work and sacrifice of others. Seeing myself as part of a continuum, I was not apart from, or separate from, other people. Those who analyze and critique officeholders observed that I was not a politician's politician. It was said that I was not hungry enough, that I did not live and breathe politics. It is true I did not relish power. I do not particularly like the word "power," because it tends to warp the perceptions of those who exercise it. I look at the idea of stewardship as an alternative mode of thinking. It is inherently healthier, because it means living with the constant reminder that our actions occur in context of other people over generations.

By some irony, it is possible that I managed to be governor for a long time precisely because I did not have a great taste for power. At the core I always felt secure in the midst of insecurity, the way I was made to feel by my parents as I was growing up. Being secure made me willing to lose an election, and this willingness to lose, if necessary, was the closest thing I ever had to a secret for political success.

While inevitably many of my personal stories look back across an era of time, my desire to share them is driven by my fervent hope that people will use the past as a means of looking to the future. We can take pride in an era that helped to define the essence of American democracy, but the momentum of that era has wound down. We must find our way anew.

We need to clarify the nature of our contribution to the country and to the world. We need to insist that this contribution be recognized and appreciated. Hawaii is not a trivial place where people come only to have fun. Hawaii is a special place. It is truly multicultural—a word that other places are groping to define. Hawaii is more nearly a nation than any other state and, as I was to have the opportunity of saying in a State of the State address, "We are a beacon of light to all of mankind."

(Opposite page) Starting out.
(Above, top) Mother and father as they appeared when I was reaching adulthood.
(Bottom) Our two-room place at Smith and Pauahi streets, in downtown Honolulu.

(Above, top) I thought I might be a reporter.

(Bottom) My family sees me off to the army: Dad is to my right, my sister Helen to the left, then my brother James, Mom with baby June, and my sister Betty.

(Opposite page) I trained at the Military Intelligence Language School at Fort Snelling, Minnesota.

CHAPTER TWO

Growing Up

WHILE FADS AND FASHIONS ARE CAUSING EVERYONE to look more alike, Hawaii has a unique history that needs to be frequently restated lest it be forgotten. In its original status, Hawaii was a Polynesian chiefdom. After 1778, the date of the first sustained contact with the West, Hawaii became a kingdom, established by native Hawaiians and increasingly influenced by Westerners, particularly Americans. The government of the Kingdom of Hawaii was overthrown in 1893 in favor of an interim Republic, which immediately sought annexation to the United States. After an extended debate, Hawaii was annexed in 1898. From then until 1959, Hawaii was an overseas territory of the United States. An historian described Hawaii as the "last among equals," referring to our being the last state admitted to the union. It is also true that we were the first American state to put the ideas of equality and fair play to work wholeheartedly.

People of different nationalities came to Hawaii from around the Pacific and mingled in context of the promise of America. We who came of age in Hawaii took the dream and promise of America seriously. We developed guidelines for equality of opportunity that I believe are fundamental to the future of a just society—as valuable to the future of the U.S. mainland states as they are to Hawaii. We may be a small state geographically, but we are a giant in terms of human relations, human understanding, and the achievement of human dignity.

The Japanese first began coming to Hawaii in large numbers in 1885. Like my parents, most were from the prefectures of southwestern Japan. They originally intended to make money by laboring on Hawaii's plantations and then return home.[1] Many decided instead to settle, and when my father arrived here in 1919, a significant number of Japanese were leaving the relatively harsh conditions of the plantations for life in Honolulu. At this distance in time from my childhood, I can see how my life was influenced by the fact that my father tried his hand at many

---

[1]In addition to my father and mother's home prefectures of Fukuoka and Kumamoto, respectively, the largest numbers came from Hiroshima and Yamaguchi.

things, but never plantation life. I did not experience the racial stratifica-
tion of the plantation, nor the wounded feelings that sometimes resulted.
We lived among all sorts of people. Many were of Japanese ancestry, but
there were many others of widely varying backgrounds.

Because my father worked at a variety of jobs, I went to school in
several parts of the island. I went to kindergarten in the Waialae area,
east of Honolulu. I went to the first grade on the Windward side of
Oahu in the country, at Laie School. There were all kinds of children
there, and my experience of the idyllic outdoor environment would later
influence one of my major efforts as governor. I then went to elementary
school near downtown in the Palama neighborhood, which today is a
sort of legendary place for bringing different immigrant groups and
native Hawaiians together. I played with kids of varied backgrounds
without giving much thought to our diversity, because we readily did
things together. We had our scraps, but our problems were minor. The
first day at Palama a bully grabbed me by the shirt. He wanted me to
know he was the "bull" of the school, as the saying went. I took a poke
at him. We lived in Chinatown during my intermediate school days until
the war broke out.

Within our family-centered environment, institutions of Japanese
community life were mingled with the institutions of American life.
Public school was by far our most important experience, and it took the
biggest share of every day. Like most of the new Japanese generation I
went to Japanese language school after public school was over. We had
to wait for language class to start, and the class itself went on for an
hour. By the time we got home, it was around five o'clock.

I participated in both the Young Buddhist Association and the Young
Men's Christian Association. The YMCA played a vital role in providing
opportunities for people to develop their bodies and learn to get along
with others. I took part in the swimming program at the Nuuanu "Y,"
and later I belonged to a YMCA club. After that I became a "High Y"
advisor. I was forever being inspired by other people, and I thought in
my own little way I could help inspire people as a junior leader in the "Y."

Life was distinctly simpler than today. Options were fewer, and choices were easier to make. Opportunity lay in education. The basic education provided for us was adequate and, for me, fulfilling. I had good
teachers. Although some people talk about how limited our school opportunities were then, our teachers taught us reading, writing, and mathematics. The basics are very important, and that's why I feel strongly about
our school system today—what it can be and what it ought to be. If only

we could acknowledge to our teachers—as we did then—that they make such a difference, and acknowledge also that the all-important process of education happens only in the classroom between teacher and student.

People have stories about their favorite teachers. I had a teacher who has influenced me all of my life. Mrs. Margaret Hamada was my core studies teacher for two periods a day when I went to Central Intermediate, which is the school directly above today's downtown. I was her student for three years, and during those years I addressed the question of what I wanted to be when I grew up. At first I thought I might like to be a journalist. I was a reporter on the school newspaper, which really interested me, but Mrs. Hamada encouraged me to look at my options. She guided me into making an appointment with a lawyer, Arthur Trask, a member of a well-known Hawaiian family. I decided lawyers help people in trouble, and that was what I wanted to do. I was in the eighth grade when I embraced law as my goal. From that moment I never wavered in my intense desire to become a lawyer.

In my excitement I told my father. He often had said to me, "I can give you money, but you can spend it all. If I help you get an education, it will be with you forever." He was extremely happy to hear about my plan. In Japanese he told me, "*Hadaka ni nattemo*," meaning that even if he were to go naked, he would make my schooling possible. He was saying he literally would give me the shirt off his back, to which he added: "Go to it." *Gambatte.*

The fact that we had no money did not seem to be a barrier, but I had a barrier of a different kind. I had a speech defect. I lisped. I had experienced this problem in elementary school, and it was still with me at Central Intermediate—a heavy lisp. Sometimes I stuttered. I would think about sound production so much that oftentimes I would forget what I wanted to say. When I decided I wanted to become a lawyer, I talked about my speech problem with Mrs. Hamada. I told her I could become a lawyer only if I learned to speak properly. Mrs. Hamada was not a speech pathologist, but she did everything she could to help. On weekends, she had me come by her classroom on the excuse of helping her with chores. I would do a few little tasks and then she would have me read aloud to her. She also encouraged me to enter oratory contests.

We had a student court at Central Intermediate, and she helped me become a defense lawyer. After I left Central, she came to the Oahu finals of one of the oratorical contests where I represented McKinley High School. She said she couldn't believe I was the same George Ariyoshi she had first met. When I became governor more than a quarter century later, Mrs. Hamada was there. Her selfless gifts lent a special meaning to the phrase *okage sama de*.

I should mention one other educator from my childhood, Dr. Miles Cary, who was the principal of my alma mater, McKinley High School. Dr. Cary is an important figure in the experience of the second generation of Japanese Americans because of his passionate dedication to the ideals of progressive education. He was at McKinley High during the first several months of my first year, which happened to be the autumn of 1941. In my limited contact with him, he projected an excitement about what others saw as ordinary. Every time you saw him he would say, "What a beautiful day! Isn't this a nice day?"

He was like my mother in the way he seemed to be saying that life was good and precious. Miles Cary made you feel there was something so exciting about any given moment that you wanted to do something with it. You wanted to do something with yourself. After the war started, Dr. Cary went off to the Mainland. It was a mark of his deep commitment to Americans of Japanese Ancestry (AJAs) that he spent a year of the war developing education programs in a Mainland internment camp.[2]

Obviously not everyone in those early days had the qualities of the various people who inspired me, but today I am struck by the depth of commitment and durable values of those who helped me grow up. We in Hawaii were a long way from becoming the "last among equals," but in those sheltered days before the war, I think you could see the foundation of an American society that would one day be first in its serious dedication to equality.

BY THE STANDARD OF THE MANY TALES ABOUT DECEMBER 7, 1941, mine is remarkable mainly for the calmness and clarity of my parents. In the early Sunday morning of December 7th, I went to Hongwanji Buddhist Sunday School on Fort Street downtown. We went early to be the first on the ping pong table, so we got there by seven-fifteen or so. I was in the basement, and I actually heard some noise coming from above, but our ping pong continued and then we had Sunday School. I walked home down Fort Street to our place on Smith Street, and when I got home my parents told me that Japan had attacked Pearl Harbor.

My mother told us all the things we needed to do, and she was quite an organizer. She had started to get canned foods and blankets together for each of us, in case we had to evacuate. She made each of us a bag, so

[2]Poston

we could take what we needed wherever we had to go. For the moment, as it turned out, we stayed where we were, but a little later we had to move out of our place in Chinatown by order of the martial law government. Everyone of Japanese ancestry near the harbor was required to move, as well as everyone near military installations. Many years later this forced move became an issue for which AJA people sought reparation. Compared to the suffering of those who were interned and relocated during the war, it was a minor thing for us. My family was used to moving, and we took it in stride. We went up into Manoa Valley to live with our cousins, who had a banana farm.

I enjoyed the farm life, and I enjoyed my cousins. We did not lack for opportunities to learn how to work. When I was fifteen, I cut *kiawe*[3] trees along the Waianae-Nanakuli Coast with a hand ax to clear a field of fire in the event of a Japanese invasion. During the rest of my high school years, I went out to work in the pineapple and sugar fields to keep the plantations going. Our work was well-organized, and we didn't mind it. We were paid fifty cents an hour.

The summer I was seventeen, I went to work in the pineapple cannery, which then was standard fare for kids in Honolulu. The first year, I worked in the storage warehouses of Dole Cannery. The cans were carted to us on pallets, and our job was to stack them up and store them away while they cooled. Then we would get an order from the labelling department saying they needed so many cans, and we would hop to it. We carted the order to the quality-control testers, who checked to see the cans of fruit were in perfect condition. The best quality controllers could tell if there was a flaw merely by tapping the can with a tiny metal device. The next summer I went to work for the California Packing Company as a timekeeper for the contract trimmers. This was a privileged position for a seventeen-year-old.

I was just young enough to miss the brunt of World War II. I was drafted just as the war in Europe ended. While I was taking my basic training, the war with Japan ended. From basic training, I was sent to the Military Intelligence Service language school at Fort Snelling, where many young men from Hawaii had trained. The role of Hawaii's Americans of Japanese Ancestry in the MIS had been pioneered by several people, including Masaji Marumoto, a Harvard-educated attorney and later associate justice of the Hawaii Supreme Court. Such other well-known people as Ralph Yempuku and Ted Tsukiyama were lifted from

[3]Known on the U.S. mainland as mesquite trees

the Army training camps, trained in language school, and sent to the Pacific, where they played roles in intelligence-gathering and interpreting. The MIS people were widely scattered by the nature of the work, much of which was classified until the 1970s. As a result the MIS did not develop the group cohesion or gain the public attention of the famous *nisei*[4] Army units, the 100th Battalion and the 442nd Regimental Combat Team. The work of the MIS was nonetheless dramatic. They saved many lives, and General Douglas MacArthur gave them credit for helping to shorten the war.

I was shipped to occupied Japan, where I spent most of my time in the ruins of Tokyo. The first Japanese person I really had a chance to talk to was a shoeshine boy at the NYK Shipping Lines Building, where I was stationed. He was seven. He told me about the suffering and the lack of food. My next meal I put some bread and jelly and butter together and wrapped it in a napkin. We were prohibited from passing food to the Japanese people, but I felt so sorry for the boy that I ignored the regulation. He put the sandwich in his box.

I asked him, "Why are you putting the sandwich away? Aren't you hungry?" He told me he was extremely hungry.

"But," he said, "I want to take this home for Mariko."

Who was she, I asked.

"My three-year-old sister," he said.

Every chance I got, I went into the Post Exchange and bought hamburgers, one for myself and one for the shoeshine boys. I was aware that I had relatives in Fukuoka and Kumamoto, but I was in Japan only a few months and had no opportunity to travel the country. I would have to wait for the discovery of much of my parents' homeland. I got my discharge as quickly as I could. I had dreamed about law school, and I was eager to pursue my dream.

When I got back to Hawaii, the veterans were streaming in, and the drinking and partying were getting into full swing. I thought if I got into that I might get lost. I wanted to go to the University of Michigan at Ann Arbor because their law school had a good reputation, and I left for Michigan without applying, let alone being accepted. Once I was there, I was told that out-of-state registration was closed but registration was still open at Michigan State in East Lansing. I did my undergraduate work at Michigan State, studied hard and gained acceptance to the University of Michigan Law School. I enjoyed my time there. Again, I had no sense of

[4]Second-generation person of Japanese ancestry

being treated differently. On the contrary, I enjoyed the fact that Hawaii had a reputation even then for people of different racial backgrounds coming together and living harmoniously.

In 1951, just before my last year of law school, my father told me about being a merchant seaman and jumping ship and living all his adult years in Hawaii as an illegal alien. I was flabbergasted. I said, "Papa, weren't you concerned during the war that they were going to come and pick you up?" He told me yes, he was, that he assumed it, but it never came to pass.

In 1952, Congress passed the Walter-McCarran Act amending the U.S. immigration law. It allowed people who could prove continuous residence since 1924 to become legal residents. In general, the Walter-McCarran Act was a step forward, in that it defined legal rights for Japanese immigrants in America, although its quota system was severely weighted against immigration from Asia. When I came home after graduation, the first thing I did after passing the Hawaii Bar was to use the Walter-McCarran Act. I legalized my father's resident status in the United States. After that he did not need to worry. For the first time, he held a passport, which allowed him to leave Hawaii and return to Hawaii. Thereafter he took many trips to Japan.

I constantly marveled at his ability to cope with adversity. When Papa was forced out of his waterfront job during the war, he went to work in a dry cleaning business. He became an expert in removing spots and stains, and he learned everything he could about dry cleaning. While I was away at school, he opened his own shop in Kalihi.

THROUGH A SECRETARY I HEARD THAT AN ATTORNEY named Fred Patterson needed an assistant, and I gave him a call. When we met, I said I felt that I had a lot to learn. I said the chance to work in his office would be its own reward.

He said, "Do you mean you're offering to come to work for me for nothing?"

I said, "Yes, for awhile."

He said, "Oh no, I couldn't let you do that, but I like your attitude."

That was how I got started in the practice of law. Where other people fresh out of law school were clerking or doing research, I was thrown directly into the fire. Mr. Patterson gave me clients and told me to come up with a plan for each one right away, which I did. One of the first things he told me was, "Go down to the District Court and introduce yourself to the people in the clerk's office. Tell them you're a dumb son-of-a-gun and you don't know anything about law practice and have a great deal to learn, and tell them you would like their support and assistance when you have anything before the District Court." I didn't tell them I was a dumb son-of-a-gun, but my conversation with them worked wonders. When I looked through the files they would say, "Don't do that. Call us, and we'll help you by telephone." I went to the other courts and repeated the same process, and it turned out to be one of the best things I ever did.

People will be tremendously supportive if you acknowledge their skills and treat them with respect and courtesy. The top administrators in institutions may change, but the staff people are there year after year. They will give you information, get you into the right places, and help you avoid mistakes. Inevitably some of the individuals at the lower levels will rise to the top. They will remember that you appreciated them "back when," and that you didn't suddenly begin to pay attention to them as they rose through the ranks.

ONE NIGHT SHORTLY AFTER I GOT BACK from Michigan, a friend of mine invited me to a party at the university. A group of young women from a Japanese sorority, *Wakabakai,* also had been invited. Someone had told me about a girl named Jean Hayashi, so when we were introduced I recognized her. I was kind of a shy guy, but as she was getting ready to leave I asked whether I could steal a dance with her. We danced, and that was the start of it. I called her right after that and asked her if I could take her to a Cherry Blossom ball.

I quickly learned that she was not only beautiful but highly intelligent as well. She had a double major, mathematics and speech. For a woman to seriously study mathematics at that time was a rarity, but Jeannie was taking such advanced math courses that she was studying with engineering students, nearly all of whom were males in those days. While she was doing fifth-year work for her teaching certificate, she taught a speech class at the university as well. She also was a mistress of ceremonies on a weekly television program called Club International, a local talent show. These were the beginning days of broadcast television, and it reflected her ability to proceed on an uncharted task confidently while helping other people be comfortable and enjoy themselves as well. She even had me on the show eating saimin noodles as part of a commercial, unpaid. We became engaged in time to experience my first step into politics together.

CHAPTER THREE
A Democratic Revolution

IN TODAY'S SOCIAL AND POLITICAL CLIMATE, people often seem to feel their lives are out of control. People talk about trying desperately to gain power, about empowerment, and "organizing." You also hear it said, "Why bother? My vote doesn't count." There is an intense frustration with the democratic process. You hear it said of people in office, "They're all a bunch of crooks." This is frightening, because it suggests people are retreating from the best form of government ever devised.

I had a very different experience, because I was fortunate to become part of the Democratic Party campaign of 1954, an event which has been elevated to a mythical level in Hawaii's history. I had been back from law school only a short time, and I was troubled by what I was seeing from my vantage point as a young attorney. I had grown up with my pleasant idea of Hawaii, and I had gone off to the Army and college without experiencing any negative incidents. But when I returned to Hawaii as an attorney I realized there was a subtle but seemingly immovable barrier above me—above "us." We could expect to go only so far. Your success did not depend on what you knew, or how capable you were, but on who you knew. I was dismayed, because this was not what I had been led to expect of Hawaii.

The controlling group often has been described as a white oligarchy, but such a description is too simplistic. It was a plantation-based society that did not exist for the benefit of the common man, but for the benefit of the owners. It excluded the great majority of people of talent and dedication from its rewards, merely because of the circumstances of birth and economics. This great majority included virtually all non-white people. Caucasians who were outside the controlling group—who were not well-connected—were often kept from advancing as well.

In the making of modern Hawaii, the year 1954 is always described as a great turning point, but that description is the result of hindsight and the writing of history. As the election season approached, there was —to my knowledge—no great sense of change in the making. In people's memory, Hawaii had always been run by the Republican Party. The

Republican Party was the party of those who had overthrown the Hawaiian Kingdom and then participated in annexing Hawaii to the United States. The Republican Party usually elected Hawaii's non-voting Delegate to Congress, and it controlled the Territorial Legislature. The Republican Party stage-managed who would be appointed governor of Hawaii under Republican presidents of the United States. Under Democratic presidents, the same privileged circles seemed to have considerable influence as well, if less directly. Even the appointed Democratic governors were on the conservative side. They did little or nothing to nurture the growth of a grassroots Democratic Party. There were some courageous Democrats of that time who fought lonely battles. We owe a debt to them, but they consistently squabbled among themselves and fell short, and Hawaii went on year after year as a U.S. territory, denied Statehood and dominated by this web of political and economic interests.

I got involved in my first political meeting through a personal friend from boyhood, Tom Ebesu. Tom invited me to go with him to the Nuuanu YMCA, which was a fitting place to get together, because some of us had grown up attending programs at that "Y." I remember clearly that the meeting was held only three days before the close of filings for the primary election of 1954. This was remarkable because it shows how spontaneous our actions really were.

Tom Ebesu said he wanted me to meet Jack Burns, the former policeman who had become chairman of the Democratic Party. Burns was to become a towering figure in the history of Hawaii, and my life was to become slowly enmeshed with his, but at the time I was merely a young person just out of school. I was twenty-eight years old. Burns had worked most of his adult life as a policeman, and in 1954 he was forty-five.

In the meeting, Burns asked me a lot of questions about what I saw going on in Hawaii. I told him I did not like the way opportunity was controlled by the select few. I said not everyone was being treated fairly. I said it wasn't how good you were at doing something, but who you knew. I said this problem wasn't limited to the Orientals or any particular racial group. It applied to the Caucasian person as well, because the Big Five controlled Hawaii, and you could only advance if you were "in" with them.

At a certain point in the meeting Jack Burns looked my way and said, "You should run for office."

I thought he was talking to someone else. I turned around to see if there was someone behind me, but no one was there. He fixed me with a look and said, "You should run for office."

My response was, "I'm too young. Nobody knows who I am."

He said, "It's not the age. It's the heart. It's how you feel."

He was insistent. "Run for office this year, and there'll be some other people running with you." He was clear about not waiting.

I went home. The next day, Tom Ebesu came back with nomination papers, and all the required number of signatures were on it. He said, "Let's go file." I was shocked. I told him, "Tom, I'm not prepared for this."

Tom suggested we talk. We went to Ala Moana Park and bought a plate lunch, and we sat looking out at the ocean. We sat for about three hours and talked about our childhood and growing up, and about how nice it would be if we could have the kind of Hawaii as adults that we experienced when we were youngsters. We talked about things that needed to be done to create a better future.

When we finished, Tom said again, "Let's go file the papers."

By now this was the next to the last day to file, but I asked Tom for one more day. In my conversations with my parents, they encouraged me to run. If I wanted to do it, they thought there was a place for me. My parents told me not to be concerned about being too young, or lacking experience. They said, "It is not age, but it is how a person is, and what a person does." The next day Tom came back again, and I agreed. We filed the papers at nearly the last possible moment.

By that time, it was only thirty days until the primary election. We used up a lot of those thirty days trying to figure out what to do. One day we were walking down the street, and we ran into one of the veterans of the 442nd Regimental Combat Team, Matsuo Takabuki. Tom had been a precinct captain two years earlier in Matsy's successful campaign for the County Board of Supervisors, and Tom introduced me to him.

Matsy said, "You're that young kid running for the House."

He invited Tom and me up to his office and talked about how his campaign had been laid out. He generously shared what he had learned.

Those were the days when we only had two House of Representative districts on Oahu. My district ran from Nuuanu Avenue in downtown Honolulu all the way to Waianae and Nanakuli on the Leeward Coast, up the plain to Wahiawa, and back down the Windward side to Kaneohe. So we had a huge district. Campaigning meant going house to house, passing out brochures, and speaking at rallies.

I threw myself into the campaign with determination. As those few short weeks progressed, everybody was amazed at the effort my group of amateurs put together. Other than Tom Ebesu, nobody had any experience, yet in a short while we had an army of people canvassing, passing out the brochure and talking up the campaign. I was thrilled. From the beginning, my father was there hard at work, going out every day door to door. My mother was really active in the campaign too. They would go out in the morning and distribute brochures and put up posters, and in the evening meet me at rallies, which then were held almost nightly. Jean was already campaigning too, tacking up posters around rural Oahu.

We had thirteen Democrats running in the primary, with six to be nominated as candidates in the general election. On primary election night, two old-timers, Charles Kauhane and Steere Noda, came in first and second. I was third. This was encouraging, but you have to remember that we still expected that Republicans would win a majority in the general election. We were living in the last few days of the Republican Party's half-century control of Hawaii, but we had no way of knowing that. We just campaigned every day and hoped for the best.

The primary is always on a Saturday. The following Monday we got together for a Democratic Party meeting, which was held in an office where the State Capitol is now located between Punchbowl, Hotel, and Beretania streets. Tom Gill, another young attorney who would become well-known in the party, was the coordinator of the Oahu campaign. Tom convened the meeting and announced we would all work together —meaning the fourth district House candidates would work together, the fifth district House candidates would work together, the Senate candidates would work together, and so on. When the candidates from my district got together, Charley Kauhane took over, as he was inclined to do if he could. Charley Kauhane was of the old school, and he was shrewd and tough.

He brought a man named Castner Ogawa from the International Longshore and Warehousemen's Union (ILWU). For those of us who lived during that era, the ILWU is such a familiar set of initials that it seems strange to explain their importance, but many young people and newcomers today know little or nothing about the ILWU. The words "longshore" and "warehousemen" reflects the union's West Coast history of organizing on the waterfront, but in Hawaii the ILWU became more than a waterfront union. It became a Hawaii-wide union that spread from the docks into the plantations, as well as pineapple canneries and other job sites in the city. The ILWU in those days called itself the One Big Union. It was militant, idealistic, and left-wing. The ILWU was a prime target of the anti-communist crusade that had divided Hawaii, and that had divided the Democratic Party, and that was always used against us in our attempts to achieve Statehood. The ILWU had been smeared with a broad brush, but they had led the unionization of Hawaii, and they commanded the deep respect of working people. Historians have concluded, pretty convincingly, that some of the ILWU leadership had been influenced by communism, but they were in the process of being pried away from the Communist Party to become participants in our democratic movement.

You might imagine what an uneven process this was, and I was right in the middle of it, trying to set a course of action. I was only beginning to learn about the political arena, but I had the unwavering support of my family and friends and the daily companionship of my father. I knew that many of the union's members unquestioningly voted the union line, and an untried candidate for office thought twice before disagreeing with the ILWU.

While I would eventually come to work constructively with various outstanding and responsible leaders from the union, I have to say that the ILWU leadership in the early days harbored a distrust of candidates they did not control. They had a reputation for being dictatorial because of tactics such as occurred in the meeting. Charley Kauhane and the ILWU representative announced again that all the candidates were going to campaign together. I said that was OK. Charley announced we were going to have team brochures, which likewise was OK, but their next line threw me. We were not to have individual brochures.

I said, "Let me see if I understand. You're saying I can't have my own literature?"

"No individual brochure," Charley said.

I asked why.

Charley said, "We campaign as a team, we push as a team, and everybody shares this team brochure. We will get in as a team."

I told him, "I can't make it, because nobody is going to know me. All your names are familiar, but mine is not."

"Well, that's the way it's got to be," he said.

I said my workers wouldn't have enough to keep them busy, alluding to the fact that I had a campaign group that I thought was as big as all the other campaign groups combined. I went to the extreme of offering to turn a page of my brochure over to my Democratic running mates, but Charley didn't buy any of it. He turned to the ILWU man and asked, "What will happen if people don't go along?"

The ILWU man said he would have to dump anyone who didn't go along. Our meeting broke up, and Charley and the ILWU man pressured me further to change my mind. I still told them no. My father told me, "Never mind, we'll go out and work extra hard." I could readily follow my father's advice. I always carefully listened to what he said, and I did not feel compelled to build a political career. I did not have to win at any price.

Matsy Takabuki came to my aid again. He assigned his brother to take me around the Waialua Plantation area. He brought in more of his key supporters in plantation areas such as Ewa and Waipahu. This was crucial, because at the time the plantations still encompassed many voters, and the ILWU was strong there. I was grateful to Matsy, because I had not previously been acquainted with him, and he had no personal connection to me.

Election campaigns are gruelling, but they can also be exciting. Traditionally campaign rallies had provided an opportunity for people to get together, and this was still true in the early campaigns. There was a serious side, which resulted from the constant speech-making and the mingling of people to talk politics. The rhetoric could be overblown, but the process gave people a general picture, and people seemed to thrive on community events. Hula and music added color, and the excitement came to a peak in a suspenseful process on election night. The ballots were counted by hand, and the running tallies came in unevenly as they were reported on a precinct by precinct basis. Town precincts tended to come in first and then the country precincts. Because voter returns varied widely from one precinct to the next, candidates could seem to be far behind and then make dramatic gains and go ahead to win.

Voter turnouts were phenomenally high, and the press covered politics in minute detail. We had a tremendous sense of the importance of elective politics. It was not something we took for granted. We were going someplace. We who were Democrats were looked on with great favor by the public, and generally officeholders of both parties were looked up to with much more respect than today. Political leaders were genuinely much closer to people then, and there was a deep sense of trust between the voter and the elected official. The cost of campaigning was nominal, and we had not felt the corrosive effect of large-scale fundraising and campaign contributions.

My own campaign media, I remember clearly, consisted of a brochure, poster, and card. Before the primary election, I paid $17 for a newspaper advertisement. It was two columns wide and three inches high. I paid another $17 for an advertisement after the primary and a third before the general election, which meant my total mass media budget was $51. We silkscreened our own banners and otherwise did everything we could to control out-of-pocket costs. Our other costs ran $154. I think our total cost was less than $500.

In this first campaign, the conflicts over relationships among the Democratic candidates went down to the wire. Charley Kauhane and the district team came back around and agreed to me exercising my right to pass out my own brochure. I compromised by agreeing that in the last week we would pass out only team materials, and that on election day we would pass out only a team card. Election day arrived quickly, and there were thousands of people out around Oahu—often passing out cards almost right up to the voting booth, in ways which are prohibited today. I went around the island to visit my campaign workers, and my first stop was Kaneohe.

My uncle, who was passing out team cards, said, "Let me have your individual card."

I said, "No, no—we can't do that."

He said, "Everybody else is doing it."

"They're not supposed to," I said.

He said maybe they weren't supposed to, but they were. I said maybe they didn't know about the agreement.

He said, "That can't be, because one of them is the campaign manager of a candidate, and another is the brother of the candidate." So I went up to this fellow and took his hand and turned it over, and sure enough my uncle was right.

At the next precinct in Waiahole, Hiram Kamaka—who was soon to be a House member himself—was campaigning for me. He told me the same thing. In Wahiawa, Jean was campaigning with her family. She said the same thing. Everyone wanted me to abandon our agreement but I said no, we would stick to it, and we did.

On election night, I was one of twenty-two Democrats who took over the thirty-member Territorial House. We even defeated Hiram Fong, the incumbent House Speaker, in what would be the only electoral loss of his lifetime. We gained control of the Senate as well, by a margin of nine to six. When I looked around, I saw people who were to become nationally and internationally known. Others were to serve admirably and well with only modest recognition, but they were mainstays in the process of changing Hawaii. Many of these new legislators were veterans. World War II—war in general—is an awful tragedy, but it had helped catalyze this great change. If something good can grow from tragedy, it happened here in Hawaii. For the first time, the majority of people had a true voice in their government, and a new direction was set for Hawaii.

I was the youngest among those who won office, but this wasn't an issue. I was grounded in a sense of what I wanted to happen in our community, and there were a lot of people who wanted to go in more or less the same direction I did.

WHEN I LOOK AT YOUNG CANDIDATES TODAY I am troubled by the elaborate nature of the political strategies that often seem to be required to even win a House seat. Their campaigns are all-consuming tasks, which go on for many months and sometimes for over a year. Today's campaigns are horribly costly in both time and money. The outcome seems to have taken on a personal make-or-break quality, but the public significance seems only vaguely defined or lacking.

In this present-day context, the fact that the 1954 campaign was so spontaneous seems remarkable. The fact that it was so brief and inexpensive likewise seems remarkable. The fact that I had no idea about making history also stands out for me. What we were doing simply seemed like the right thing to do.

Life was amazing. Jean and I went through the 1954 campaign together, and the next year we were married.

CHAPTER FOUR

The Use of Power

THE QUESTION OF WHO WINS AN ELECTION often is more exciting to the public than what the winners do with the office, but what is done with public office is the more important question. It's one we must get back into focus if we are to really restore the good health of our public life.

My intention here is not to recite the details of the 1954 movement through time, nor to unduly dredge up names and political labels. But events occurred along the way that illuminated the issue of accomplishment versus aggrandizement.

Our agenda for change can be briefly stated as opportunity and equality. We sought to improve education at all levels, and to create new possibilities in higher education. We wanted to create a more equitable relationship between business and labor. We also promised land reform for the individual homeowner.

I remember saying to myself, "We've talked about equal opportunity. We've talked about letting each person rise according to ability. How do we make that come about?" I searched to define more clearly what we intended to do, and how we would do it. Now that I was elected, what was the point of victory?

I personally decided I was not going to do what *they* had done to us. If we took the power of office as an excuse for shifting benefits to our friends, we would merely be doing the same thing the Republicans had done. I didn't want to take anything away from anyone. I didn't want to redistribute favor or riches. Instead, I wanted to create more opportunities so that an ever-growing part of the population could participate in the benefits of society.

The question was whether we would be fairer and more far-sighted than the individuals and the party we had defeated. Would this dramatic electoral change prove to be a victory of idealism and principle? Or would it merely result in the creation of a new in-group? I spent a lot of time thinking about this. I struggled with it. When this reflective process was finished, I felt clear and settled.

From the beginning we were plagued by factionalism within the

Democratic Party. Factions sprang up around strong individuals and around labor unions as well. A schism between the Neighbor Islands and Oahu played a part. To some extent, issues divided people into factions, but beneath the surface there often was raw grasping for power. We Democrats were *often* in danger of losing to in-fighting what we had gained at the ballot box. If you read *Hawaii Pono* by Lawrence Fuchs, you will be vividly reminded of the role factionalism played during the early years of that highly charged political environment.

The first session, the speakership went to my Fifth District running mate, Charley Kauhane. At one well-publicized point in the session, Charley stopped the clock of the session by taking it down from the wall of Iolani Palace and putting it in the trunk of his car. His core support was a group of seven Democrats. There were also eight Republicans in the House, which added up to fifteen people, or half of the House. The rest of us were inexperienced Democrats. We had the jitters, wondering if Charley might put the clock back up and run the session in our absence. As a result we hung around the chamber in shifts. We wouldn't leave for lunch until Charley and the Republicans had left. People know me today as calm and controlled, but in the 1955 session I had a reputation for being a scrapper. Fellow legislators fed me ideas on ways to do battle with Charley, but this was a role I realized I wasn't really comfortable with, and I let it go.

In 1957, a battle broke out for the speakership. Dan Inouye had been majority leader in 1955 but in 1957 he approached me to support him for speaker. He seemed confident that he had the votes, but when the time came I was one of only three House members voting for Dan. We took him aside and said he had to work on his vote-counting skills, which he obviously did, because he became a renowned United States senator. At one point Spark Matsunaga became so frustrated by the maneuvering and wrangling that he swore he would never run again, but he managed to endure his frustrations. He became a long-time U.S. House member and then an outstanding United States senator along with Dan Inouye.

For the purposes of the 1957 session, O. Vincent Esposito was elected speaker and Elmer Cravalho was elected chairman of the House Finance Committee.

In the excitement and confusion, I don't remember being discouraged. I did not then, and do not now, see people as perfect. I didn't have to see everything happening at once. If I could see some progress, I felt we were moving in the right direction. At that point we were still a territory under the Republican Administration of Dwight D. Eisenhower, and naturally the governors he appointed were Republicans. There was a conflict in viewpoints, and much of our legislation initially was vetoed.

In the 1954 election Jack Burns ran for delegate to Congress at the last minute and lost by a thousand votes. During that campaign he came around and watched as my father campaigned on my behalf. Nobody in politics knew my father before the 1954 election, but during the 1954 campaign my father was all over the place. He spoke little English. "My boy, my son," was often about the limit of what people understood from him. Nonetheless Burns used to chat with my father, and he recruited Papa to be one of his campaign workers, and to carry his brochure along with my own. Burns was careful to speak with me and say that he was only asking for help from my father, to convey that he did not want to dilute the overall effectiveness of my whole campaign team. When Burns ran again for delegate to Congress in 1956, he won a landslide victory.

By this time the country was actively debating the issue of Statehood for Hawaii and Alaska. Most people thought Statehood would be granted first to Hawaii and then to Alaska, because we in Hawaii had been kept waiting since 1898. There is an interesting picture of the 1950 Constitutional Convention of the Territory showing a banner that says "49th State." A book was written called *Hawaii, the 49th State*. We had the 49th State Fair, businesses called 49th State such-and-such, and even a 49th State Bar. Despite this optimism about the likelihood of achieving Statehood, deeply-rooted factors stood in the way. The radical element of labor was always cited by opponents as a reason to deny us Statehood. The racial makeup of Hawaii was still a factor, and so was the certainty that we would become a strong civil rights state.

What Burns did with the maneuvering for Statehood put him in a new and even better light for me. He knew he had the 1958 election coming up (Territorial delegates, like voting House members, were elected to two-year terms), but he nonetheless supported the strategy of allowing the Alaska Statehood Bill to be voted on first. He knew that if Alaska got in, we were certain to get in as well. Alaska became the 49th State instead of Hawaii, and Jack Burns' career was nearly ended. When he came back for the 1958 campaign he pledged that if his strategy did not work he would never run again. It took a lot of courage. I thought to myself, "This man really believes in getting something done, and he's willing to sacrifice himself politically to do it." Congress's vote for Hawaii's Statehood in 1959 proved Burns right. After that, whenever I needed to do something I felt was right, I thought of the example set by Jack Burns.

In the 1958 election, I moved up to the Territorial Senate, and in the following special election for Statehood I easily held on to my new position. In the 1959 legislative session, I became enmeshed in a conflict that influenced my perception of public life. Although I had won in 1959, the Senate had fallen back into the hands of the Republican Party by a margin of fourteen to eleven. In the same election Burns lost the first governor's race to the incumbent presidential appointee, William F. Quinn. It was the one point in Democratic Party history when it appeared the pendulum was swinging back to the Republican side. In the aftermath, Quinn nominated Samuel P. King to be a judge. Sam King was the son of an appointed Territorial governor, Samuel Wilder King, and he had been a somewhat partisan chairman of the Republican Party during the 1954 election.

However, Sam was known as a smart, good-natured person and a good attorney. When his nomination was sent down to the Senate for confirmation, a couple of Republican senators declined to support him, so he did not have the required majority of thirteen votes. The Democratic caucus met and discussed the situation. Most of the senators thought it was a great chance to embarrass the Quinn Administration and the Republican majority in the Senate. All we would need to do was stick together, eleven strong, and we would dump the Republican governor's nominee, who happened to be not only the past chairman of the Republican Party but also the son of the Republican governor prior to Bill Quinn.

After everybody got through talking, I asked one question, "What kind of judge would Sam King make?" They all told me he would make a good judge, but they said that was not the point. I asked, "What is the point? Aren't we talking about whether the person is qualified?"

Finally one of the senators responded: "No, this is politics. If we stick together, we can really embarrass the Administration."

I asked, "What about the person? What are we doing to the person? If that person is someone's husband, someone's father, someone's son, do we not destroy the life of a person by doing something like this?"

Nonetheless, the feeling was, "Well, tough, he just happens to be there, and we have to stick together."

I said I had listened carefully to everything they had said, and now I wanted them to listen to what I had to say. I went back to when I first met Jack Burns and to when we talked about the ceiling that limited our opportunities in life. "Everybody was treated okay up to a certain level, but beyond that level opportunity was always reserved for someone who happened to be a friend of someone in a high place. Unless you had that kind of connection, you could not break the barrier." That was why I agreed to run for office. That was why I wanted change. "Now you're asking me to do what I felt was so wrong. Now we're going to say that Sam King shouldn't be a judge simply because he is not our friend, and we're going to hold up his nomination."

I told them it would be a beautiful testament to our philosophy if we could say instead, "He may not be our friend, and we did not have to support him, but we stand for the idea that we should play on an even playing field. A person should be rewarded because he is talented and qualified and not because he is someone's friend." People were getting angry, but I went on: "It is so easy to stand up for principle when the principle works in our favor, but we've got to stand for principle when it's not working in our favor."

I would like to say I changed everyone's minds, but I didn't. I left the caucus and called Sam King. I told him I was going to vote for him, which gave him all the votes he needed. He became a good judge and, eventually, an outstanding judge of the Federal District Court. What happened that day was a further step in practicing what I had been taught from an early age, which was to listen carefully to others and try to find a common ground, but to go it alone if necessary. Because I was the type of person who tried to accommodate others, such disagreements did not come easily or naturally.

I should also say that how such disagreements are treated in the aftermath can be as important as the disagreement itself. One way is to publicize disagreement, which has the effect of sensationalizing and usually worsening the situation, solidifying bad feelings. My response was to minimize the disagreement, to not dwell on it, and to avoid the temptation to wring some short-term political advantage from it. I ignored it and got on with my work. Jack Burns used to say that you should never think of anyone as a political enemy. "Someone who is your enemy today may be your friend tomorrow." I agree.

In 1970, I would play a fundamental role in helping Jack Burns defeat Sam King for the governorship, yet Sam and I remained on good terms. In 1984, he was invited by the Chamber of Commerce to deliver a speech on the life of a Federal judge. He looked my way and said, "In my first appointment, I didn't have the votes to be confirmed until I received a call from a Democrat saying he would support my confirmation. That Democrat happens to be the governor of Hawaii." A few weeks later I ran into him again (after not seeing him for years). I said,

"You might as well know the rest of it." So I told him what had happened in the Democratic caucus.

WHEN I'VE BEEN ABLE TO HELP COOL TEMPERS and create calm, I have tried to do so. But in the partisan and faction-ridden environment of the early years, this was all but impossible. In the 1962 election, Jack Burns defeated Bill Quinn for the governorship. The Democratic Party also recaptured its majority in the Senate after three years of being in the minority.

In broad outline this completed the Democratic drive to take control of the government and attempt a transformation of Hawaii into a progressive new state based on the principles of equality and opportunity. This broad vision was more easily described than accomplished.

Despite my break with the Caucus over Sam King's judgeship, I was elected chairman of the Senate Ways and Means Committee. This is a challenging task, because you must go over the condition of the economy, projections of revenues, the tax structure, and what the governor and fellow legislators propose to spend. You must question hundreds of witnesses. You must facilitate the committee members getting all their questions asked, apportion time, and balance innumerable petty conflicts by exercising what you hope everyone will see as fair procedure. This cumbersome process must move forward within the constitutionally allotted time for a legislative session.

Most important of all, you must actually know what you're talking about in order to make responsible decisions.

Chairmanship of the Ways and Means Committee, along with chairmanship of the House Finance Committee, is probably the most pressure-filled job in the Legislature. It also is a great way to learn about every aspect of State government in considerable detail. The chairmanship had particular meaning in 1963 because it was the first year in Hawaii's history that an elected Democratic governor, in the person of Governor Burns, had responsibility for management of governmental finances in conjunction with a Democratic Legislature. How responsibly we performed would set a pattern for the future.

In the 1963 session of the Legislature, we had a ten-member Ways and Means Committee. Because the Democrats now controlled both houses of the Legislature and the Executive Branch as well, expectations ran high. Nonetheless, money was not unlimited and the budget had its own realities. I remember Governor Burns sent down a budget of $131 million. We turned out to have $118 million in tax revenues and about $12 million in fees, so we had to struggle to keep the budget in balance.

We shifted money around to give more funding to education, which required that we cut the governor's budget in some areas. Despite this further increase in education, several of my Democratic colleagues were not satisfied. I said that everything we cut elsewhere we could put into education, but we could not pretend to spend money that wasn't there.

In the search for a financial plan in which total expenditures matched total revenues, many people argued that money would appear as revenue which we had not anticipated. At one point I was told to make earnings from Hawaii's participation in the 1964 New York World's Fair part of the revenue projection. I declined. It turned out that the Hawaii pavillion cost money rather than making money.

We came down to negotiating a financial plan with the House, and the pressure was building. From among the members who were demanding a bigger education budget, one came back at me and restated the demand. This was Patsy Takemoto Mink, who soon was to develop a national reputation as a U.S. congresswoman and an advocate for education. She said that even if we could not balance the numbers she wanted more in the education budget. I restated my position, which was, "We have to deal with the realities of the numbers as they exist." Finally we got so we could make no more cuts elsewhere, so I told the House and Senate conferees that we had talked long enough. We needed to make decisions. I was adamant that we not pass a bloated budget just to say we had provided money for education. It would make the Administration look bad when it could not actually spend that amount of dollars.

Mrs. Mink said if I was not going to change my position she would walk out. For various political reasons a second Democrat, Nadao Yoshinaga, known to everyone simply as "Najo," joined her. Then a third senator, John Ushijima, joined Najo in the walkout. The committee's hard work was in danger of collapsing. I was fearful that a freshman senator from Maui named Harry Field would be the fourth walkout, because he had been elected with a lot of help from Najo. I liked Harry Field. We used to have Ways and Means meetings in the morning, afternoon, and evening, and around ten o'clock at night Harry and I would stay and talk about the budget. He would ask, "This thing I heard today—can you explain it?" Every day I spent time with him going over the substance of the money issues before us.

When the three members walked out, I asked Harry in for a special meeting. I said, "I know Najo helped you get elected, and if you feel you have to walk out too, I will understand."

He looked at me and said, "Najo helped get me elected but you taught me everything I know about the budget. Every question I had, you answered. I know where we are, what the problems are, and why you can't give more than you've already given. From what I've learned, I know you're right. I'm sticking with you." Harry was a former football star, a huge, strong guy. He grabbed my hand with his enormous hand and squeezed vigorously.

A second senator, Benjamin Menor, came in.[5] He too could have had some reason to walk out, because we had been on opposite sides in organizational conflicts. Instead he said, "Enough is enough. You've been willing to take the rap when you didn't need to. I'm sticking by you." He and I developed a close working relationship and we became close personal friends.

The senior Republican, Randolph Crossley, also came by. He told me he appreciated I had treated him fairly and equally, and he appreciated the fact I had not been partisan. He said he too would stick by me.[6]

I went to the Legislature on a Monday morning and went into the House-Senate conference at the Board of Water Supply building on Beretania Street. I went home that night only to shower and change, and this continued through Thursday evening. I rotated my team of negotiators on behalf of the Senate, but I myself participated virtually all the while. A year later Ben Menor told me that on Thursday, while he was acting chairman, I had fallen asleep in place for nearly two hours. I didn't remember it. Probably I thought I had only blinked, but it was proof to me that the human body can take only so much. On Thursday evening we successfully concluded the House-Senate conference along the lines of our position. We finished our work with seven functioning committee members and got the bill passed.

SHORTLY AFTER THE 1963 BUDGET FIGHT, Harry Field fell ill. Because we had become close, I was permitted to visit him frequently before he passed away. He was courageous, intelligent, and caring. If he had lived he would have been one of the leaders of modern Hawaii.

He was married to Kapiolani Kawananakoa, a direct descendant of Hawaii's last royal family. I became acquainted with her and other family

[5]Ben Menor eventually was to become the first Supreme Court justice of Filipino ancestry, one of my many appointees to the bench.

[6]Randolph Crossley was to run against Jack Burns for governor in 1966 and against me in 1974.

members and we talked about the idea of forming an organization to restore Iolani Palace and make it a museum. Subsequently I did the legal work, without compensation, to form the Friends of Iolani Palace, which has cared for the Palace ever since the State Capitol was completed in 1968. I think of that sometimes when I think of Harry Field.

THE 1963 SESSION WAS IN A STATE OF CONSTANT CONTROVERSY. It became best known for the battle over what was called the Maryland Land Bill. That name may lack meaning for many people today, but the underlying land issue is still with us. It has to do with the fact that in ancient Hawaii, land was held on a use-right basis but was not owned. As Western influence grew, the Hawaiian Kingdom adopted an ownership system as a result of what was called the Great *Mahele* (the great division). Enormous parcels went to a few people. Much of it passed from Hawaiian hands into Western hands, but some of it was retained as an asset for Hawaiians in the form of trusts, of which Bishop Estate—which supports the Kamehameha Schools for native Hawaiians—was the largest. Most land in Hawaii was owned by a relatively few entities. As the population grew, housing was built on land that was leased for long terms but not sold outright to homeowners. People owned their home structures but not their home sites.

The early-day Democratic Party had promised land reform, which meant using the power of government to transform leasehold home sites into fee simple ownership. You can imagine how emotional the issue of land reform can be.

Initially there was no great push for land reform in the 1963 session. Within the Senate, we had a party program, with legislation assigned to one of three levels of priority. The Maryland Bill was priority number three, but various influential legislators and labor union people seized on it. Suddenly it became a big priority of the 1963 legislative session.

The Maryland Bill, as it was drafted, had a serious flaw that few people understood. Our constitution protects contractual rights, and existing leases are a form of contract. Therefore the "reform" legislation could not tamper with existing leases. We could not give an option to existing leaseholders to buy their land. We could only give that option to people who were renewing their leases, or buying new homes on lease land. To me this meant we were headed for creating two categories of people living side by side, one with an existing lease but no option to buy, as contrasted to one with a new lease that carried with it an option to buy. In economic terms, I believed the existing leaseholds would become so unattractive to potential buyers that the market values would plummet—and with market values would go people's life savings. In social terms, I was concerned that we would be creating two different classes of people living in the same neighborhood.

I asked numerous questions about this feature of the bill. I became painfully aware that most of the public and most of the Legislature thought the Maryland Bill would allow everyone to buy their land, period. The Maryland Bill was perceived as a simple answer to a complex problem. Nelson Doi, who then was president of the Senate, came to me and asked that I keep an open mind. He urged me to not disclose a position, hoping I would come around to supporting the bill. A deadlock developed at twelve votes against twelve votes, and it was my job to cast the deciding vote.

A message came down suggesting that I might lose the chairmanship of Ways and Means if I did not go along with the Democratic Party position. Since Ways and Means was such an important committee, people might well have thought this threat would bring me around. When I received the message saying, "Come along or you might lose your chairmanship," I said by way of reply, "Come and replace me if you want to."

I received so many telephone calls at home that I asked friends over to the house to help out. I did not want to have my wife Jean cope with all the calls herself. Some of my friends came over, and one night they had twenty-seven calls, all trying to put pressure on me. Some of these were nasty, with people swearing into the telephone.

The unions demanded to know how I was going to vote. Two of the top leaders of the AFL-CIO came around and talked about how many members they had, and how their members would take it out on me if I didn't go along. I kept telling them, "Don't give me those numbers. They're not of interest to me. I'm trying to resolve this thing in a way that will be fair and workable, and all your numbers will not help me solve this matter."

They came back and said, "We have ten thousand members." I told them, "You see that door over there? If you mention your membership one more time, you can use it."

I voted no on the Maryland Bill, and it died.

The criticism was thunderous. I had to wonder if my career in politics was over. In the process I learned that Governor Burns actually agreed with my vote. He called and said he was pleased to see me take the position I had. He said it required courage to stand up for what I felt strongly about, and furthermore that I had saved him the trouble of vetoing the bill. He reinforced in me the idea that you don't always have to be a part of the group, and you don't have to do what other people do.

In late spring of 1964, with the election season approaching, I gave a speech to the Japanese Chamber of Commerce. I said if I was reelected I would continue to oppose the Maryland Bill. I said that if legislators merely followed party platforms "we could go into session for about six days—introduce the party bills, pass them in three days in the Senate, and another three days in the House, and send them to the governor for signature, with no need for hearings."

I contrasted this mock scenario to my real conviction that every bill should be given a hearing and every legislator should "vote his conviction."

The 1964 elections put my particular convictions to the test, because feelings were still running strongly against me. I went to a rally in Wai-pahu, a strong plantation community and a strong union community. People I was acquainted with were afraid to shake hands with me. Sometimes they were visibly anxious when I approached them, and they folded their arms over their chests. I gave up trying to shake hands with people in the crowd and waited my turn to speak. My statement was possibly startling in its brevity, because I had a simple message I wanted people to think about. I said, "If you want someone who is a rubber stamp, you shouldn't vote for me. But if you want someone who will study an issue and then vote according to conviction, I hope you will consider me." I felt people were listening.

One of my fellow senators told me not to talk about the Maryland Bill on the campaign trail because it embarrassed him and other Democrats. "Just talk about being chairman of the Ways and Means Committee, and you'll get reelected," he said. I didn't think it was right, nor was it politically smart, to avoid the issue. I wanted to explain my position to the voters but I didn't want to embarrass my fellow Democrats, so I said, "I won't do anything to hurt you folks, so you won't see me at the party functions. I'm going out on my own." I asked all my friends to organize coffee hours where I could sit and talk with people in depth. I tried to do two coffee hours a night for thirty straight nights. Sometimes there would be twenty-five people and sometimes several times that many. I imagine I talked with an average of a hundred people a night.

When I would finish talking, many people shared their thoughts—often after the sessions were nominally over. One group said they did not realize what the bill was all about, and their anger turned to gratitude. They said, "We didn't understand it, but now we do. We thought everyone was getting a right to buy their leasehold, but now we see we were going to get hurt." These people wholeheartedly agreed with my position.

A second group remained opposed to my position but became supportive of me anyway. They liked the way I came to my conclusion. They appreciated the fact that I was willing to stick by my convictions under pressure. They liked my willingness to come back and talk about the controversy in detail. They said in essence, "Although we disagree with you, we think you're the kind of person who should go back and serve us." Only a few remained adamantly opposed to my position and to my reelection.

I learned something indispensable that I hope young officeholders of today will consider. When voters realize you have carefully studied an issue and arrived at an honest judgment, they may vote for you again in spite of your specific position, provided you care enough to talk straight. People are looking for leaders who will do their homework, exercise judgment, and vote their convictions.

The depth of communication that occurred in these coffee hours was another turning point in my political life. I saw more clearly that people look for values, belief, and commitment. I saw that if a fraction of the people were really with you, and understood why, it could ripple outward through many voters.

By speaking with a hundred people a night for thirty nights, I directly reached about three thousand people. I told people at the coffee hours that I was only reaching a small percentage of voters. I asked them to go out and talk about the exchange of views, either for or against me. I suspect many went out to speak family to family, friend to friend, and neighbor to neighbor on my behalf, because on election night I won easily. I waited for the Waipahu precincts where people had greeted me with their arms folded. I was happy to see I had carried those precincts.

BY THIS TIME I WAS THIRTY-EIGHT YEARS OLD. I had won office six times. I had carried a special weight of decision-making as chairman of the Ways and Means Committee. I had regrouped sufficiently from the Maryland Bill to be elected Senate majority leader for the 1965 and 1966 sessions. I was accumulating a valuable political education, but I had no particular ambition beyond what I was doing. Much of my time and energy went into the practice of law, which was what I wanted.

After practicing with Fred Patterson, I joined a firm with three other young lawyers. One was Russell Kono, who had been in the Military Intelligence Service in the Pacific. Russell was one of those elected to the

Territorial House in 1954. A second was Alfred Laureta, who would become the first person of Filipino ancestry to hold a cabinet-level position. Later he was a State judge and then a Federal judge. The third person was Bert Kobayashi Sr., who was to play an important role as attorney general and then associate justice of the Supreme Court.

Politics is an inherently intense experience, but I tried to maintain some sense of balance between my law practice and politics, as well as between work and family. If I thought I could make a genuine contribution in the political arena, I did so, but I did not reach for high office for its own sake, as I think a story from the 1967 legislative session illustrates. After the Republican successes in the first Statehood election in 1959, the contending factions of the Democratic Party had temporarily put aside their differences, but by the 1967 legislative session Democratic factionalism was rising to a high tide.

Governor Burns had appointed his lieutenant governor, Bill Richardson, to the State Supreme Court, which set off a jockeying for political position. Governor Burns had turned to several different people to fill the lieutenant governorship, but for various reasons these individuals did not want to get involved. He then settled on the idea of filling the job with Kenneth F. Brown, now a well-known community leader but then relatively unknown. Brown then was defeated by Tom Gill in the 1966 election.

After I worked with Tom Gill in the 1954 campaign, in 1956 I got my first taste of his ongoing conflict with Jack Burns. Tom was running for Oahu County Party chairman, and Tadao Beppu was also running for chair with backing from the Burns people. At that time I wasn't considered a Burns man, and after Tom won the county chairmanship, I and several others thought we needed to minimize such needless conflicts in the future. I particularly recall Tom Ebesu telling me, "Let's go help now. Tom is the chairman, so we shouldn't hold out against him." My law partner Bert Kobayashi joined me in this effort. I remember telling Tom Gill that we should pull together, and I was jarred by his response. Essentially he said that because he had won, things would be done *his* way. This was an indicator of our future relationship.

In 1966 Tom was riding high politically because he had beaten the Burns candidate for lieutenant governor. Nonetheless he was still only lieutenant governor, and Burns was still governor.

The 1966 election stirred up a lot of ill feelings within the Democratic Party and among the different unions, and these feelings spilled over into the organization of the Senate. On one side were the more strongly

pro-Burns people and the ILWU, led by Najo Yoshinaga. On the other
side was a group who were more friendly with the AFL-CIO and Tom
Gill, led by Nelson Doi. Personalities and personal friendships took on
an exaggerated importance in this environment. Najo had the support of
his wartime buddy, John Ushijima from the Big Island, as well as Billie
Fernandes from Kauai. Nelson had good friends in such people as Vincent
Yano[7] and Duke Kawasaki, an ardent supporter of the Maryland Bill who
had campaigned against me.

I was elected temporary chair of the Democratic Caucus because they
saw I was the only one who was genuinely not aligned. I was asked by
both sides to join their groups, but I refused. Because of my preoccupation with keeping the process open, I did not think of myself as neatly
fitting into either group. Nelson Doi's faction offered me the presidency
of the Senate, which meant I could have a large office, a large staff, and
the potential for media coverage that politicians often seek. I turned
down the presidency because it would have meant the Yoshinaga group
would have been shut out. I said I would accept it only if we could reach
a genuine compromise on chairmanships and committee assignments.
The Senate presidency did not have the power to hold people together
from above, and a real compromise was required. When I turned down
the presidency, I realized I was headed for oblivion, at least for awhile.
When the deal was finally struck, the two factions took the key positions
and I was relegated to the chairmanship of the Public Utilities Committee, which was one of the least glamorous tasks in the Legislature. If you
want to talk about prestige and influence, I had gone from the top of the
heap as chairman of Ways and Means and then majority leader to somewhere close to the bottom.

It didn't particularly bother me. I did my job. A sincere new senator
named John Lanham was chairman of the Lands Committee. He wanted
to pass a land reform bill, so he came to me and said, "George, what is
your real problem with the Maryland Bill?"

I said I was for conversion from leasehold to fee simple ownership
but it had to apply fairly and equally. In fact I had informally helped
facilitate a voluntary conversion process. This eye-opening experience
had arisen after a trustee of Bishop Estate Trust had asked me what I
wanted to see done.

I told him the Estate should voluntarily convert as much land as they
could from leasehold to fee simple. Bishop Estate owned Halawa Heights

[7]Yano was eventually to be my competitor in my campaign for lieutenant governor.

and wanted to use that as its demonstration project. The Estate trustee asked me if I would help. I told him, "I don't want to be hired as a lawyer, because then I'll be tainted. But I want to help, so I'll get the community to hire a lawyer." The community got a young lawyer named Harry Masaki, who lived there, and I sat down and talked with him. I said I could talk to Bishop Estate, and that both sides could come to me for help on those points I felt strongly about. I said I wanted voluntary conversion, so that we could start a process wherein many neighborhoods could convert from leasehold to fee simple. I told the lawyer to organize the community, and we would bring the two sides together.

I made it clear I was not getting anything from Bishop Estate and did not want anything from the community. This helped me be effective. The community voted to convert and got reasonable prices.

From this experience, the idea of communities getting together and letting everyone have a chance to convert became essential to my thinking. I told John Lanham that a conversion law had to include everyone in a given community equally. The landed estates had legitimate concerns as well. One was that under voluntary conversion their income was fully taxable, which meant they would lose a good deal of their assets to taxation. John and I talked, and we said, "What about condemnation at fair market value?"

Together John and I came up with the Leasehold Conversion Act. Because I was well-known as an opponent of the Maryland Land Bill, my support for the Leasehold Conversion Act made a lot of people feel comfortable, and it passed the 1967 Legislature. Governor Burns allowed the Act to become law, but he was always wary of it, and nothing was to be done with it until I became governor myself. At that point I found an executive named David Slipher who had extensive experience with Kaiser Development Corporation. We got people organized and the process going, and thereafter the act was widely used to facilitate leaseholders buying the land on which their homes were built.

In many ways the land reform embedded in the Leasehold Conversion Act of 1967 was the last major step in the process of the Democratic Party delivering on its promises of 1954. Impatient people may ask why it took so long. People who look at broad movements in history may marvel at how quickly such far-reaching social and economic change occurred.

IN TIMES TO COME, WHEN I WAS THE SUBJECT of increased scrutiny, I was often described as a middle-of-the-roader. I would concur in a general way, because I am a consensus-builder. By turning down the Senate presidency, I turned away from merely holding office for the sake of holding office. I knew that the makings of a real working consensus among us were lacking, and this was proven time and again as our proceedings disintegrated into acrimony. Bringing peace to the off-and-on factional fighting among the Democrats was beyond me. I focused my energies where I could make a genuine contribution.

The Senate underwent such stress in the 1967 and 1968 sessions that it was extensively reorganized for the 1969 and 1970 sessions. David C. McClung lined up the votes to be president. He came to me and expressed his appreciation for the way I had handled my role as chairman of the Public Utilities Committee. He said I easily could have become a thorn in the side of the Senate leadership, but I had refrained and worked cooperatively. He offered me any one of three positions, my old job as Ways and Means chairman, majority leader, or majority floor leader.

I said I would work wherever I could be the most useful, and left the decision up to him. I became majority floor leader. It is a good job to have if you want to attract attention, but it also is a good job if you want to improve the overall workings of the Legislature. Some people have used it to function as a sort of talking chief, but I took the opposite approach. I undertook to see that action on the Senate floor was managed smoothly and properly, that legislation moved to the floor only when it was ready, and that if problems with legislation were identified on the floor they were resolved. I would go quietly to a committee chair and suggest remedial action, and the chair would take it from there.

I tried to build consensus, minimize conflict, and maximize constructive work. If something needed to be said on the floor, I went to committee chairs and encouraged them to take the spotlight and do the speaking. I was very quiet, and I think those two sessions operated better as a result.

My father often had talked with me about the concept of *otagai*, referring to the profound value that Japanese place on mutuality. At the same time he had admonished me to not fear taking my own course: *"Do the things that are right. Never mind what happens thereafter."* I feel that in those legislative years I put those seemingly paradoxical ideas to the test. On the one hand I was very much a team player, but in extraordinary instances I was willing to be the odd man out and go it alone. For those individuals who would later attack me as a "machine Democrat," which to me connotes being a follower in a crowd, I would suggest they look back to the times when I stood alone.

(Preceding pages)

I'm here with my dear friend and mentor Tom Ebesu on my immediate left. Our friends provided a ready base of support, even though we were inexperienced.

(Right)

The 28th Legislature, 1955.

Front Row: Hon. Esther Richardson, Steere Noda, Elmer Cravalho, Speaker Charles Kauhane, Daniel Inouye, Manuel Paschoal, Anna Kahanamoku

2nd Row: Toshio Serizawa, Toshiharu Yama, Manuel Henriques, Akoni Pule, William Fernandes, Sumio Nakashima, myself

3rd Row: Raymond Kobayashi, Stanley Hara, Russell Kono, Spark Matsunaga, Peter Aduja, Masato Doi, Nadao Yoshinaga, Yasutaka Fukushima, Joseph Garcia Jr.

4th Row: Philip Minn, Thomas Miles (Ass't. Clerk), Robert N. Kimura, David Trask Jr., E.P. Lydgate, O. Vincent Esposito, Robert Hind Jr., Hebden Porteus, James Woolsey Jr. (Sgt.-at-Arms)

(Following pages)
With Jack Burns.

Inauguration days start in Iolani Palace.

CHAPTER FIVE

With Jack Burns

IN 1969, BETWEEN CHRISTMAS AND NEW YEAR'S, several people called on me to discuss running for lieutenant governor. One was Bert Kobayashi, who by then had been Burns' attorney general for two terms of office. The second was Eddie DeMello of the ILWU. The third was a man named Nelson Prather, a lobbyist for the sugar industry.

I was surprised. I had never thought about such a thing. My first response was, "How does Governor Burns feel about this idea?"

They told me, "You'll get a call from him."

They had no sooner left my office than the telephone rang, and the governor asked if I would join him early the next morning at Washington Place. Over breakfast he reiterated what Bert Kobayashi had said, that he wanted me to run for lieutenant governor. I told him that running for higher office was not something I had given much thought to. I said I already had put in many years in the Senate. I was thinking about one more term, which would give me twenty years in the Legislature. By then I would have done my part, and I would become a private citizen.

The governor said he wasn't thinking so much about who would run with him in 1970, but who would succeed him in 1974. He kept on talking about 1974. I kept telling him, "Governor, I'm having a hard time thinking about 1970. Please don't ask me about 1974."

He said, "Okay, as long as you don't say no for now."

FIFTEEN YEARS HAD GONE BY SINCE GOVERNOR BURNS had recruited me to run for the Legislature. He had not only taken an interest in me but in my father. I had been inspired by the way he handled the Statehood Bill in Congress. As Ways and Means chairman I had taken some criticism to pass a budget that stayed within what the State could afford. I had taken a lot of criticism over the Maryland Bill, saving him the problem of vetoing it.

However, I was by no means a part of Burns' inner circle. My closest link to him was Bert Kobayashi. Bert and I had tried to mediate the con-

flict between Burns and Gill in 1956, and after Burns won the governorship, the first person he brought into his cabinet was Bert Kobayashi,
even though Bert was not a member of his political circle.

I think my connection with Bert played a role in the governor's
assessment of me, because Bert was a fair-minded person who focused
on getting things done. Bert's job as attorney general was crucial because
the Democratic agenda was to break up the interlocking boards of directors of the Big Five companies. Within the small group that historically
had controlled Hawaii, influential directors from one of the companies
would sit on the boards of other companies, and vice versa. Bert had
actually worked for one of the companies and had decided that his
opportunities were limited, so he might have relished hauling the boards
of the Big Five into a bitter, humiliating court battle. Instead he negotiated an agreement that led the companies to abandon their interlocking
directorates without going to court. It saved taxpayer money, and it also
prevented further ill will.

This approach was typical of Bert, and such moves became a trade-
mark of the Burns Administration. After years of conflict, this constructive approach created a consensus over what kind of place Hawaii
should be. The very word "consensus" took on a special meaning.

As a key aspect of building the consensus, Bert served as Burns'
mediator of labor negotiations. Hawaii had a history of economically dis-
astrous strikes, and Burns, wanting to change this long pattern, kept his
finger on the pulse of labor negotiations. He commanded the respect of
labor, and also of business, which was glad to learn he was not anti-business. At the right moment, often at literally the last hour before midnight, Bert Kobayashi would step in, using Burns' immense prestige to
pull out a settlement.

While I think my association with Bert Kobayashi helped me in the
eyes of Burns, I believe it was the governor who came up with the idea
of me running with him, because he was so ready to talk about the idea
in detail—as if he had developed it himself, and not borrowed it.

BEYOND THE NARROW QUESTION of how Burns came to ask me to run, I
now can see how conflicts within our society, and within the Democratic
Party itself, had been building up for many years to set the scene for our
breakfast meeting.

John Burns was born in 1909, which made him seventeen years my
senior. He had grown up as a *haole* boy in the local neighborhood of
Kalihi, the oldest of four children, raised by a devoutly Catholic mother.

Jack Burns understood viscerally what other liberal Caucasians understood in perhaps a less basic way. He understood how hard life had been in Hawaii for the great majority of people, how limited opportunity had been, how hurtful discrimination was, and how people were held back if they were not among the privileged few.

Burns joined the Honolulu Police Department in the 1930s as a way of supporting his own growing family, and in the hope it was a system in which a person rose on ability rather than through social contacts. As the war with Japan threatened, he was assigned to head something called the Espionage Bureau of the Honolulu Police Department. In that capacity he worked with the Federal government's intelligence agencies on the question of whether people of Japanese ancestry in Hawaii would be loyal to America in the event of war. As a result of his ease of communication with Hawaii's people, Burns knew that we who were of Japanese ancestry were overwhelmingly loyal to America and to American ideals. Burns knew this from experience, and he knew it in his heart. He played a unique role because he addressed the question of loyalty as a Hawaii resident at a time when the national government was looking at us all with such intense suspicion.

When I got involved in the Democratic Party in 1954, there were some older Japanese who still believed that Burns had spied against the Japanese. They said he was an *inu,* a dog. When I think about the things that happened, I know this whispering against Burns was wrong, and that in a real sense he had put himself on the line for people of Japanese ancestry.

He had to have had a real conviction to speak up for AJAs at that time. After he had assured everyone that the AJAs were completely loyal to the United States, what if there had been some kind of incident? He would have been held responsible.

After the shock of the Pearl Harbor attack, Burns was involved in helping maintain morale within the Japanese community, and then with organizing the 442nd Regimental Combat Team. As the war went on, he worked with a circle of associates who began to map out how the Democratic Party could be a vehicle for transforming Hawaii.

It is true that in Hawaii's political history Burns happened to be in the right places at the right times, but that observation says nothing. In the challenges he faced, he responded intelligently, courageously, even-handedly, and with the right mixture of passionate commitment and stoic resolve. He did not waver.

He was a deeply religious man as well as a pragmatic political leader. Perhaps for both those reasons he said that you should never treat anyone as an enemy. *"Someone who is your enemy today may become your friend tomorrow."* He had fought the ILWU's attempts to take over the Democratic Party, and he won his battle against the ILWU. At the same time he argued the case of the ILWU with the national government. As a result, the ILWU gave up their efforts to control the Democratic Party and where he might have made an enemy he made a friend. By the time I met Burns in 1954, he was regarded as a tough and determined organizer, but support for him was far from unanimous.

Even in those early days, the patterns of the key personalities were set. Tom Gill became the focal point of the opposition to Burns and the alternative to top leadership of the party. Frank F. Fasi also was active at this early stage and quickly became known as an inventive political campaigner. Both had sharp tongues and were adept at using the media. Of the two Tom Gill was the more consistent and, I would say, the more purposeful. Gill was a war veteran and a labor lawyer. After the Oahu campaign in 1954, he became an attorney for the House of Representatives. He won election to the House in 1958 and became immediately embroiled in a fight for control. He wanted his friend Vincent Esposito to be speaker and he wanted to be chairman of two key committees, the Judiciary Committee and the Lands Committee. This struck many people as a way for Tom to push through land legislation singlehandedly, avoiding an appropriate deliberative process. Perhaps Tom thought of it as efficient. At any rate he had a good deal of support, but he overreached. He lost that particular organizational battle and, eventually, the battle over land legislation as well.

As I've said, Tom Gill tended to believe the way to do things was his way. He played an important role in developing the early platforms of the Party, and a substantial number of Democrats came to believe that Tom's way was right. He was the attorney for many of the AFL-CIO unions, which frequently fought with the ILWU over jurisdictional issues, so the possibilities for conflict within the Democratic Party and the unions were wide-ranging.

Sometimes the Burns and Gill factions would pull together at election time, and sometimes they wouldn't. Working together produced victories. Not working together resulted in recrimination. In 1962, Robert C. Oshiro, who then was a young State legislator, pursued a long, tedious process of putting together a unity slate to pull the factions together. The process helped. That was the year Burns was elected governor. Tom Gill was elected to the U.S. House of Representatives, but two years later he lost a race for the U.S. Senate to Republican Hiram Fong.

Those were the years of the Great Society programs of President Lyndon Johnson, who was a good friend of Burns and a good friend of Hawaii. Burns gave Tom Gill a job implementing the Equal Opportunity Act in Hawaii. The goal of the Act was to put an end to poverty in America, and for a brief optimistic time in the middle 1960s this seemed like a credible goal. However, the Vietnam War was escalating, and with it a climate of conflict.

The issue of who would succeed Burns as governor first came up in this context. When he had tried to bring Kenny Brown into the picture to succeed Chief Justice Bill Richardson, Tom Gill had stood in the way, much to Burns' dismay.

I personally believe that after the 1966 primary election Burns went through a period in which he was willing to lose the general election rather than see Tom Gill run with him as the candidate for lieutenant governor. Despite his own reelection campaign, Burns took an assignment from President Johnson to represent the United States at the independence ceremonies of the new African nation of Botswana. Botswana is on the exact opposite side of the globe from Hawaii, which provided some kind of tie-in. When Gill won his primary election campaign, Burns was so upset that he refused to return to Hawaii on schedule. At the time I was in touch with Matsy Takabuki, the 442nd veteran who had helped me win my first election. Matsy went to meet the governor on the Mainland. His message was, "We're all committed and we're all working hard for you. We want to see you be governor again, but you've got to want it too. And if you don't want it, you've got to tell us." Matsy wanted to be sure that when the governor got off the plane he didn't say something to Tom Gill in front of the press that would doom the campaign. If no one had talked with Burns, I think he would have let the campaign go and lost the election. As it was, he was visibly terse with Tom Gill at the airport. The television cameras picked this up, and the scene haunted the rest of the Democratic Party campaign. Only at the last minute did Burns and Gill and everyone else come together. They barely won, when they should have won easily.

These events hung in the air as I considered Burns' request that I run in 1970 for the much-disputed but constitutionally modest office of lieutenant governor. Tom Gill was a younger, more verbal person than Burns. To a good many people Tom seemed to better typify the style of the 1960s, and as such he appeared to be going places. The question was whether Tom Gill was moving from the success of 1966 to a takeover of the governorship in 1970. Because of the aura of victory that had resulted from 1966, it was easy to forget that Tom Gill's strengths were also weaknesses. He was articulate, but he had a habit of saying cutting, belittling things that assaulted people's dignity. He was good at describing a worthwhile goal, but he left people feeling there was only one way to achieve it.

I was perplexed. Where I had been thinking about winding down my public life, I was faced with making a full-time commitment. My family would be subjected to hardships. I was doing well in my law practice and had reached the point of being selective about who my clients were and what kind of practice I wanted. I was just putting a new law firm together through which I sought to bring many of the capable young lawyers of the next generation together.[8] My law practice would have to be closed down. I would have to go all-out in the 1970 campaign and "not say no" to Burns about running in 1974.

The idea of breaking barriers, which originally had motivated me, was an inseparable part of my considerations. The new State of Hawaii had produced United States representatives and senators of Caucasian, Chinese, and Japanese ancestry, reflecting our diversity. But only Caucasians had been governor. Lately a writer has described as ironic the fact that Burns as a white person led the 1954 movement, while most of the votes came from non-whites. My own view is that sometimes it is easier for somebody else to tell you that you or your group can do better than you're doing. It carries more weight if someone from another group makes the case, because it is not as likely to be dismissed as biased. Burns tended to validate us.

When Burns had first run for governor in 1959 his running mate was Mitsuyuki Kido, a prominent member of the Japanese community and one of the original founders of the Democratic Party. Burns and Kido lost to the team of Bill Quinn and James Kealoha, who were respectively Caucasian and part-Hawaiian. Then Burns and Richardson, Caucasian and part-Hawaiian, came back to win. There was a subtle connotation that an old pattern was being unwittingly perpetuated, in which Caucasians ran the show, part-Hawaiians played supporting roles, and AJAs stayed a certain distance from the top. Now, with Gill as lieutenant governor, both the top positions were held by Caucasians, and it seemed Tom Gill might be governor far into the future.

[8]The nucleus of this firm eventually divided into two large firms, currently known as Watanabe, Ing & Kawashima and Kobayashi, Sugita & Goda. I take pride in having brought them together and in my association with them.

Burns thought it was important to break the barrier, not just for the Japanese but for all minority groups. I think he felt that if I could become governor then a lot of people would be able to say, "We can take off all the constraints. We can dream, and we can feel that Hawaii is the place where we have unlimited opportunities, a place we can become anything we want to become."

Burns felt that if we did not make the breakthrough, there might never be a governor of non-white minority background. He told me how badly he had wanted Mits Kido to become lieutenant governor so that Kido could move on to become governor. Because that didn't work out, Burns felt that perhaps 1970 was the opportunity for me to move up to lieutenant governor and then look at the governorship in 1974.

Some people asked, "Why Ariyoshi?" When people look back, I may seem like a logical choice, but it was not that simple at the time. A person such as Mits Kido had been through the inner workings of the war experience while I was a teenager enjoying life at McKinley High. Kido was of an earlier generation. By several years, I had missed the experience of the 442nd with which Burns was so heavily identified. The 442nd group had been preoccupied with the issue of loyalty, and their legend revolved around that theme. As a result of the war, they developed a tremendous cohesion and direction. I felt my own experience was inferior to theirs, and what they had endured. I felt a great debt to them and what they had done to make things easier for those of us who followed. At the same time, I was different from them. I was the youngest of the 1954 group, and I had to be myself.

I announced my candidacy in early May, after the Legislature adjourned and just as the campaign season was starting. I made it clear I was not in this merely for my own sake, but I was supporting Jack Burns for reelection. By July, my campaign group had organized a big fund-raising dinner that really got the energy going in my campaign. When it was my turn to speak at the dinner I addressed my children, Lynn, Ryozo, and Donn. At the time they were nine, eleven, and thirteen. I was concerned that they be part of the campaign and also that they understand the pending change in our family life. I told them they were fortunate to grow up in a community that is committed to human dignity, "where there is equality of opportunity, and where you can dream, and dreams become real if we work for them."

Many people did not like to remember that "we didn't always have equality of opportunities, and people were not always advanced in business on the basis of their abilities."

I said if any single individual deserved credit for the great changes that had occurred in Hawaii it was John A. Burns. I believed deeply in what I said, and people caught the spirit of my conviction. Through this speech, which I repeated many times through the campaign, I tried to get the longer and most pertinent span of history clarified in people's thinking.

I threw myself into the campaign. I may not have had a reputation for being a particularly political person, but I work hard. For me campaigning was no different from doing any other job. I felt I had to do it in the right way. I had to motivate people to come out and work for me. My friends told me I was at my best in smaller groups and coffee hours. I felt it was particularly important for me to get a hard core of people who believed in me, and who would go out and do all the time-consuming things that must get done. That's the way I had built up my campaign team. Every campaign I added new people who felt strongly about things that I believed in, and this had put my campaign team on solid ground.

I was particularly fortunate to attract supporters who did not specifically want anything for themselves. They didn't try to dictate to me. What they said to me was, "We believe in you. Give us your best shot." These were people who looked at events over longer time periods than from one election to the next. They had a deep belief in the importance of the future. They were willing to make sacrifices in the present so the future could be better. That kind of support made it possible for me to do my work.

I had a clear field until just before the filing deadline, when the Gill campaign put up Vincent Yano, a colleague from the Senate. The usual thing in such a contested race would have been for me to ensure my own election by running as a neutral on other races, then form a ticket with whomever won. Instead I continued to campaign for Jack Burns, because I believed his reelection was much more important than my own election. I threw my effort behind Burns with no political strategy in mind other than to help him. It did not appear to be a politically smart thing to do at the time, but it would turn out to be so, because Burns never forgot my unreserved commitment to him. When I first announced my support for Burns, he was roughly two-to-one behind Tom Gill. Although Burns' people mounted an enormous campaign for him under the leadership of Bob Oshiro, the outcome was unclear down to election day.

I have reason to think Burns felt he would lose. After the last rally in Hilo, we stayed overnight on the Big Island and came back to Oahu in the morning. It was the day of the primary election. The governor was picked up at the airport and gave Jean and me a ride home. In the car, he shook my hand. His last words to me were, "You're going to make it, but I'm not sure I'm going to." He had never said that, and it really touched me. I felt sad, because I realized that was the way he must have been feeling during the entire campaign, thinking that his career was very possibly going to end in defeat.

When the returns came in that night, he won by a surprisingly wide margin, and I won by a wide margin. Now he and I were formally and officially the Democratic nominees, a ticket and a team.

The Republican primary nominated Sam King, who I had supported for a judgeship eleven years earlier. His running mate was Ralph Kiyosaki, who was known for his service as superintendent of the Department of Education. They presented an attractive opposition ticket, but Burns and I were a logical, compatible pairing. We were comfortable with one another.

What Burns had proposed to me just after Christmas in 1969 came to pass on general election day, 1970. He was easily elected to his third term as governor, and I was elected lieutenant governor. I turned to the future with a sense of excitement. I had a deep sense of obligation to do well, and I was determined to give meaning to the office. Little did I know how much I would be called upon to do.

DURING CAMPAIGNS THERE IS OFTEN AN EMPHASIS on the two-person ticket, but only the person at the top of the ticket governs. The two offices on the top floor of our Capitol are of equal size, but all the constitutional authority and responsibility lies with the governor. This means that the lieutenant governor's real work—or lack of real work—depends on the governor. Not surprisingly, subtle conflicts and often open antagonisms have developed between the two offices, notwithstanding the statements about teamwork that are made during campaigns.

Republican Bill Quinn had a falling out with his lieutenant governor, James Kealoha. Burns had his problem with Tom Gill. I was to have my own problems later as governor.

However, this decidedly was not the case between Burns and me. All the good will, hopes, and dreams we previously had experienced only served to enrich our working relationship as governor and lieutenant governor. It is a simple, historical fact that Governor Burns and I had by far the most constructive, positive relationship of any two people to hold our respective offices. From the beginning, he was deeply committed to developing my understanding of the executive branch of government. Right after the 1970 election, he made me the head of his cabinet. I called all of his cabinet meetings, and I worked closely with the departments.

I personally held meetings with Governor Burns on an average of several times a week, and sometimes daily. Often these were impromptu. They could take up an entire day and go on into the evening.

He would call me about ten or eleven in the morning and ask whether I had anything scheduled. I would say no, I didn't. If I did, I would rearrange it. I would go over and have lunch with him and spend all afternoon with him. Fairly often our conversations would run on into informal dinner at Washington Place.

During this period I sat through many of his conferences. When someone had an appointment with him, the governor would say I was going to be sitting with him. He was exposing me to the way in which a governor must be involved in so many things in the community. He was trying to accustom me to the role. If anything of importance happened in my absence, he would call and tell me what was going on. I was seeing at close hand the person I had known for many years at a distance. In a close, daily view I felt as positively about him as I had before.

At the beginning of our term he was sixty-one years old. He had been the most important force in molding the modern Democratic Party. As delegate to Congress, he had gained passage of the Statehood Act for Hawaii. He was known in Washington as the central figure of the Fiftieth State. He had close relationships with key figures in Congress, both Democratic and Republican. With the help of Lyndon Johnson, he had started the East-West Center for international academic exchange in the Pacific. He had enjoyed a special relationship with the White House when Johnson was president. By now he was in his third term as governor.

He could have taken the attitude that he had done it all. He was an imposing figure, but he approached our relationship with an enthusiasm that affected me deeply. While it was true he could be very dominating, he made a great point of avoiding that mode of behavior. He always stressed to me the importance of everyone being their own person, and of every individual making a unique contribution.

Despite the amount of time he spent with me, he was not trying to cast me in his mold. He was saying my style was not his, that inevitably I was different, and I could not effectively do things the same way he did. I would have to do what felt right to me. He always told me, "Remember you're different from me, and you're more effective doing things your own way than trying to do them my way. You have your background, and I have mine. Do whatever you have to do in the way you can do it best."

As a result, I knew that in my assignments all I had to do was think things through and be myself. Regardless of the outcome, he was not going to get upset.

One vivid illustration was a situation on the Big Island where one of the plantations was dumping the refuse of sugar cane (bagasse) over the cliff into the sea. The State was becoming increasingly conscious of the environment, and the State Department of Health issued notice that the sugar company must desist in six months and spend a large sum of money on alternative practices. I talked with Burns about the seriousness of this conflict between economics and environmental practice, and he said, "Why don't you take a look at it and come back with a recommendation."

I recommended a longer grace time, with the idea of helping the sugar company ease the transition and channel their environmental investment into not only cleanup but the generation of energy by burning the bagasse. Burns said, "You're going to get a lot of criticism." Sure enough, I got a telephone call. The deputy attorney general on the case had resigned and gone to the U.S. Environmental Protection Agency charging I had made a "sweetheart deal" with the plantation.

Burns and I had a meeting. He asked what I wanted to do in light of the bad publicity. I said, "It was the right thing and I want to stick by it."

He told me, "If you can stand the heat, work it out."

My approach took several years, but we got the ocean cleaned up and added to the power supply of the Big Island at the same time.[9] I could not have done this if Burns had not supported me. I think his support reflected an appreciation for other people taking responsibility and exercising judgment.

On a philosophical level, this concept of people being themselves and making their own unique contribution is central to my story. It is the essence of the Democratic Party's contribution to Hawaii and, I think, to the world. It is an infectious attitude. Burns, as a person with strong views who had been through many battles, could have ended his career as an autocrat. Instead he rededicated himself to helping others.

He often expounded on the idea of including as many people in the political process as possible. The test was not those who had supported you but those who had opposed you. He told me, "Don't paint anybody

---

[9]This non-oil source met about one quarter of the Big Island's energy needs.

into a corner. In a state like Hawaii where personal relationships are so important, if a person has to go campaign and get involved in the other side, it's okay. Circumstances sometimes make that necessary. Maybe the person is married to someone on the other side. You can't expect to create friction in the family by that person campaigning for you instead of for your opponent. You've got to be big enough to understand that. Circumstances may change, and the next time that person can become part of your group."

Don't lock people out. Be open. I know for myself there were many people who strongly opposed me for whatever reason, but who later became supportive of me.

I GRANT YOU THIS VIEW OF BURNS may surprise people who remember him as surrounded by individuals whose watchword was loyalty. It is true there were individuals around Burns who were poised to say, "Oh, that guy was not with us, so he's out." A demonstration of loyalty to the United States was the test to which so many had sacrificed themselves in the 442nd. Loyalty is a strong traditional value of people generally, and this is so with those of Japanese ancestry. I had my own definition of loyalty, which I construed as loyalty not only to individuals but to principles, and our foremost principle was openness and fairness.

I wish I could find the speech I gave to the 1972 Democratic Party Convention, in which I called for genuinely opening up the ranks to newcomers. I talked with Governor Burns beforehand about that speech. I told him I was going to say we had to change. He smiled. He didn't say whether I should or shouldn't make this speech. He wouldn't say whether he was for it or against it. I had gotten to understand him well enough to know his silence meant, "You've got to do things on your own."

I often spoke without a text, but I carefully wrote out my speech calling for openness. I got halfway through the speech and turned the page to find the last four or five pages were missing. Wow, what a feeling! I ad-libbed the conclusion. The Democratic Party was at a critical stage, and it had to change.

A few years earlier, Bob Oshiro had made a chart that showed the ages of all the people in the Legislature. It showed how they had started off young but their average ages had gone up and up. We were in danger of being an aged party unless we brought in new people with new blood and new ideas. I believed we could not just tell new people to come in on the condition that they listen to us. There were other people who were giving lip service to the theme of openness, but I was saying, "The difference between you and me is you still want to retain complete control. You don't want to let these new people have any real influence."

We were saying to these new people, "Come in. The party belongs to you." And then we were treating them almost like robots. They were coming to precinct meetings and being told how to vote. Sometimes they were given slates. The process of control began at the precinct meetings, because typically no important issues arose and the only real question was who would go to the State convention.

When people arrived at the Democratic Party convention they were told what to do, and they were expected to follow marching orders. Treating people like that was, in my view, deeply insulting.

If you really wanted people to come in, you had to tell them, "Come, use your best energy and your best judgment, and do what you feel has to be done." I think the role of leadership is not to control but to promote an understanding of our philosophy and what we are trying to accomplish in the community. Leadership means truly treating people with dignity and practicing respect for the individual.

The underlying meaning of my speech went to the issues of who was chosen for party positions, and how decisions were made, because at that time the delegates to the National Democratic Convention, as well as key offices, were chosen by a small group over Sunday breakfast.

The speech was coldly received by some old-time Democrats. They felt I was destroying the Democratic Party, but in later years I was actually able to make the changes I proposed. By making my speech early in my term as lieutenant governor, I think I was being faithful to my relationship with Governor Burns as well as to my beliefs. The issue *always* was what we do with our so-called power.

IN 1971, A FEW DAYS AFTER MY FORTY-FIFTH BIRTHDAY, my father said to me in Japanese, "Oh, you've become a man now." It is kind of odd to hear that translated into English, but I knew it was a pronouncement of his confidence in me. He used the words "*ichinin mai ni natta*," meaning I had become a full person, that I had reached my potential and had become an adult in a real sense. He said I would continue to grow, that I had a great deal more to learn and do and accomplish, but he was satisfied. My father was also saying he was convinced that the next time around I was going to become governor.

My birthday is on March 12, and I think we had our conversation shortly after that, on March 14. He usually did not go to Japan until around June, but that year he went right after our conversation, because his brother was having his sixtieth birthday party and wanted him there. Papa caught a cold. It got much worse, and he was put in Kumamoto University Hospital. My mother called me to come see him. When I got there the doctor told me it was too bad I had come so far. He wanted me to understand my father would probably not know I had come.

When I went in there, my mother told my father that I had come. I bent over and said, "Papa, can you hear me?" He gasped and said yes, *hai*. He put his arms up and put his hands around my neck, and he pulled me toward him.

The doctor was watching. He said, "You must be very close to your father. If I had not seen it I would not have believed he could do that."

A trade mission from Hawaii was headed for Tokyo. The governor was to have headed it but could not, so he had asked me to do so. I told my mother I was going to cancel my involvement with the trade mission, but she insisted that I not. She said, "You're not a private person now. You're a public person. I understand that, and Papa understands that, and if he felt that because of his condition he kept you from discharging your public responsibilities, he would feel terrible. You've got to go." I went to Tokyo to meet the group as they came into the airport, and I was with them for the business meetings. Then my mother called me to tell me that my father was not doing well at all. I couldn't get a flight out, so I took the train. A distant relative met me at the station and told me that my father had passed on. Later he said when he saw the reaction on my face he felt terrible, and that he never wanted such a responsibility again. When I saw my mother in Kumamoto, I started to say, "I shouldn't have gone," but she stopped me. "Don't say that. You did the right thing," she said.

We brought my father's body back to Hawaii and held his funeral services here. When he first had seen Hawaii he had said, "This is nice, I think I'll stay," and his life turned out to be an amazing saga.

I THINK THAT AS WE APPROACH THE TWENTY-FIRST CENTURY, it is important for people to understand more about the early 1970s, because many of the problems that surfaced at that time are, much more clearly, becoming the problems of today. For the purposes of this story, it is necessary to understand the changing climate in which Governor Burns and I were working.

In retrospect the 1950s and 1960s form a sort of golden era in the minds of many people. The drive for equality and equal opportunity was substantially successful. Hawaii became a state. The world was fascinated with us. The traditional economy of Hawaii began to diversify and grow, supported by a long period of national economic expansion. The death of President Kennedy cast a shadow over the country, but the passage of Lyndon Johnson's legislative program made it seem that great achievements had resulted from the tragedy of Kennedy's death.

Governor Burns believed deeply in consensus. Lyndon Johnson believed in consensus. There were years in the 1960s when people in Hawaii seemed to be unified around goals, and the country also seemed to be unified around goals. Then, more than anything, the Vietnam War changed the political and social environment. It resulted in a climate of antagonism and mistrust. This was as true in Hawaii as it was around the rest of the country.

Many new problems and issues arose at this time in addition to the Vietnam War, and pre-existing issues became more obvious or acute. In a short time span, people became much more concerned about air quality and traffic congestion, and likewise about water quality and the long-term availability of water. Drugs became a problem during these years. "Hippies" descended on Hawaii. Native Hawaiians began to get in touch with a lengthening list of grievances. The large amounts of money required to run political campaigns became an issue. Japan had begun to invest in Hawaii, and there were enough sales of real estate to Japan to generate a negative reaction. The old economy of pineapple and sugar was slipping, but people weren't that happy with tourism as a replacement. The cost and availability of housing was a chronic problem. Underlying this climate was an uncertainty about the basic health of the economy, after a period of rapid economic growth.

As the year 1973 went on, Governor Burns did not feel well. He was hospitalized on Oct. 16, 1973, and an operation followed. He was diagnosed as having cancer. I was thankful for all the background he had given me, because I increasingly had to assume responsibility for managing the State government. Where Governor Burns often had made the point that I was George Ariyoshi, not Jack Burns, skeptics now said the same thing with a different intent. One publication described me as "a practiced follower," indecisive, and generally not up to the task. I was not the great figure of history who people had come to rely on.

More and more I was hurrying back and forth between my office and Burns' office, not to meet with him but to take his place. It fell to me to manage the budget in the face of rising costs and uncertain tax revenues. The governor's response had been to put a freeze on hiring new people. If a vacant job was to be filled, he had to personally approve not only unfreezing the job but filling the position. This was a two-step process across his desk, as well as across the desks of the hiring department and the State Personnel Department. It consumed a huge amount of time. I also felt strongly that it misplaced the decision-making responsibility. I believed State government had become so complex that no one person could understand that level of detail. The governor often needed the advice of the Department of Budget and Finance, and in effect the budget analysts were making decisions on how a department was going to function. All the other departments had fallen into the habit of passing the buck to the governor's office. This meant to me that the department directors were no longer doing their jobs by making the hard decisions.

I issued a memorandum fixing responsibility with the department directors. I gave them budget ceilings and told them to live within them. Within those limits they were responsible for spending, running their departments, freezing and unfreezing positions, and hiring. This new direction had to do with my own deeply held belief that people must be given authority and responsibility in equal amounts, and they then must be respected, supported, and held accountable.

Cutting spending was only part of the budgetary problem. The 1968 Constitutional Convention had provided public workers with the right to collective bargaining, and the costs to the government were coming due. In the 1973 legislative session there was a projected deficit approaching $200 million. More money was needed to cover the collective bargaining contracts, even though the economy was not doing well. There was serious talk of a general tax increase, but I was opposed to it. I felt neither individual familes nor the economy of Hawaii could afford more taxes.

As I was struggling with budgetary issues in early 1974, the oil and gasoline crisis struck. This was an international crisis that had an extreme impact in Hawaii because of our near-total dependence on oil and gasoline for energy.

A general panic set in. People waited in line all night outside gas stations to be there when the stations opened. Fights occurred, and the public mood was not good. Politically, the opposition was gearing up its criticisms—contending that I was a weak leader and that the confusion proved it. They suggested that if I were tough enough I would crack the whip and force rationing.

I wanted to solve the problem through a community effort based on cooperation. I felt we needed to bring about some sense of security among the people and an understanding that everyone was going to be treated fairly. Everyone was going to get their fair share, whatever that was. One possible solution was to say that drivers had to use up a certain amount of gasoline before they could come in for a refill. A second was to say only half of the people could come in on a given day.

I was fortunate to have creative and capable people who came together, talked it out, and came up with a plan. Walter Dods, later president of First Hawaiian Bank, served as a brilliant strategist of communication. He headed the effort. Dr. Fujio Matsuda, who then was director of the Department of Transportation (and later president of the University of Hawaii), worked closely with Walter. The result became a graphic campaign symbolized by a new word, *gasplan.*

Gasplan combined elements of both the alternatives to rationing. First, people could not gas up unless the tank was at least half empty. This eliminated people who were in a panic and constantly topping off their gasoline tanks. Second, people could only gas up on an even-numbered day or an odd-numbered day depending on the last digit of their license plate. Monday became known as an "even day," Tuesday as an "odd day," etc.

Everyone was urged to follow these two simple guidelines and to help out by conserving as much as possible. The lines shrank dramatically and then disappeared altogether. Feelings changed almost overnight. People felt they would be able to get their share, and we would not run short as long as we acted sensibly. I think the key to success was moving people from an atmosphere of conflict to an atmosphere of cooperation. As a sense of fair play took hold, the lines disappeared.

This experience influenced my actions from then on. I had been given a quick immersion in the big-picture facts of energy and resource management. I had vividly experienced the reality of limits that had always been awaiting us all. Resources are finite, a fact so simple and pervasive that it required a fundamental shift in our way of being. I emerged from this experience determined to do my part in developing a rational, creative response. Conservation was to become an important part of all my programs, along with the development of renewable alternative energy resources.

As THE YEAR WENT ON IT BECAME OBVIOUS that Governor Burns' illness was incurable, and I officially became acting governor on his behalf.

At the point I became acting governor, the Democratic Party had been the dominant party for twenty years. The election season approached, and there was a lot of shifting around and vying for position.

Uncertainty was in the air. *The Hawaii Observer* described the Democratic goals of 1954 as being either "accomplished, forgotten or discredited," and the Democratic Party as being splintered into a half-dozen groups. I could count at least six different campaign groups myself.

Elements of the Burns group supported me, but others were slow to come around. Some turned away. David McClung, who was both Democratic Party chairman and president of the Senate, was periodically testing whether to run. Implicit in his maneuvering was a question of whether I would be a good candidate or a weak candidate. David was close to the governor, and he also had been a labor lawyer (at one time with Tom Gill), and some of the unions liked him. To tell the truth, I had moments when I thought that if Burns was so certain he wanted me to succeed him, he should let his supporters know, but he did not. The fact that David jumped in the race was a factor. More fundamentally, I realized Jack Burns, in his wisdom, felt I ought to develop my own campaign and my own strength instead of relying on his group. I think he was concerned that if I relied on his group I would not develop my own adequately, and I would not be as strong as I needed to be. I concentrated on improving my own statewide group, and I thought of getting volunteers from the Burns group as a bonus.

So there were three groups right there—mine, McClung's, and the Burns people. Frank Fasi had been mayor of Honolulu for six years and was absolutely determined to be governor. He had been waiting for his chance, and he obviously believed this was the right moment. Tom Gill still had a loyal following, and he also was determined to run again. Then Nelson Doi announced he was running for lieutenant governor in a team relationship with Tom Gill. He made all the indications that he was determined to do for Tom what I had done for Governor Burns. However, Nelson Doi and Tom Gill apparently did not get along at such close quarters, and Nelson changed his position by announcing that he was nonaligned. He was running independently of Tom or any of the candidates for governor and would team up with whomever won the nomination. So counting the Burns group, myself, McClung, Tom Gill, Frank Fasi, and Nelson Doi, there were six campaign groups at work.

The Democratic primary was do or die, and I thought I might lose. I was concerned that McClung would draw from areas that I otherwise would draw from. As acting governor I represented the status quo, and many biting and critical comments were directed my way. Frank Fasi had a strong starting position as mayor of Honolulu, and Tom Gill also got his campaign off to a good start. Both of them had a lot more experience

than I did at running campaigns for high office. I started out behind Fasi
and Gill, but I was far enough ahead of Dave McClung to establish this
as a three-way and not a four-way race. Again I relied heavily on coffee
hours and talking with people in depth, even if I did not directly reach
that many people. I set forward my vision of what Hawaii was and what
we needed to do next. I did not respond to the hits. I was positive.
Slowly things improved, and on primary election night I pulled ahead
decisively in the poll that counted. Fasi was second, and Gill came in just
behind him.

Nelson Doi was nominated to run with me as lieutenant governor.
By this accident of personalities and timing, we had gone from having no
AJAs on the ticket to having two. This didn't seem to matter. Once we
survived the primary, I felt the campaign would go along fairly smoothly, and it did. The Republicans put up Randy Crossley for a second time
and Ben Dillingham as his running mate. They represented an era that
had passed. Victory came easily in the general election.

As the first governor of Japanese ancestry, I felt a special obligation,
and sometimes a special burden. From my background, I think you can
see how the concept of *haji* came in. In Japanese terms, it was my job to
avoid failure, to not bring shame on the family or on our heritage. I had
to do well not only for my own sake, but for the sake of many others.

On election nights, Jean and I had always watched television at home
to get a feel for what was happening so we could be prepared when we
went to headquarters. That 1974 election, when I knew I was going to be
okay, I went to the Kuakini Hospital to see Governor Burns. I walked in
and said, "I think things are going to be okay, Governor, and I want to
thank you very much."

He said, "Don't thank me. I want to thank you for making my dreams
come true."

When he was taken home to his place in Kailua, I would go to see
him. Mrs. Burns took me aside and said she was no longer going to send
him back to the hospital. She was going to keep him at home and let him
go with dignity. She recalled all the times I had been to Washington
Place for dinner as lieutenant governor, and the peace of mind he had
gotten from having me on the job.

In those last days, Governor Burns couldn't talk much, and we never
talked business, but I experienced the deep feeling that existed between
us. He had been born into an almost feudal plantation society. He had
played a central role in transforming it into the most shining example of
fair play and democracy. When he was asked to name the most impor-

tant achievement of his Administration, he ignored all of his administrative and legislative achievements and focused instead on a letter he had written early in his first term. The Pacific Club, a symbol of the old order, had invited him to be a member, and Burns had written to them courteously declining. He said he could not think of such a thing until it opened its doors to all races. About a year later the letter came out in the newspaper. Suddenly the club's racial policy was reversed, as if life in Hawaii had changed forever.

John Burns had vision. He had a passionate concern for correcting injustice. He taught us, above everything else, the worth and dignity of every human being. He saw in all of us the gleam of hidden human treasure. He reminded us that we are all the equal children of a Divine Creator. He stood up courageously in the panic of 1941 when people of Japanese ancestry were in the greatest jeopardy, and he took pride in seeing a person of Japanese ancestry become governor. He passed away at the age of sixty-six on April 5, 1975.

CHAPTER SIX
Governor

NEW DIRECTIONS IN PUBLIC LIFE must be generated by candidates in the course of political campaigns. The successful candidates must outline a direction clearly and promote that direction as promised. The 1974 campaign generated a new direction for Hawaii that was challenging as well as humbling. I believe 1974 was a turning point in State government. It also was a turning point for the Democratic Party, which I believe has not been adequately understood to this day.

I want to focus on this turning point because I believe it has so much to do with how we need to manage our future. The challenge that faced my Administration in 1974 continues to face us all—in Hawaii and elsewhere—as we move toward the year 2000. It is the challenge of balancing our needs for the present with the needs of our children, grandchildren, and those as yet unborn. It is the challenge of using resources wisely.

We had to move from a politics of more and more to a politics of frugality. The 1970s brought the issue of frugality into focus, and this issue became the core of my agenda, which we worked on throughout my Administration. Frugality was sometimes discussed on a national level, usually by Jimmy Carter. But finding a new balance, reordering priorities, taking the long view over the short—these are difficult to do. Perhaps the public tired of these goals, or never wanted to face them. A false national prosperity during the 1980s, brought on by massive borrowing, may have obscured this agenda, but nonetheless it is the great reality of our time. The 1970s were a preview of the 1990s.

The energy crisis of 1972 did more than remind us that oil is a limited resource. It also got us in better touch with the fact that the capacity of our land, air, and water are limited. As an island society, we began to see, I think much more clearly than any continental state, that we had to accept a new era of limits.

The stark fact of limited resources was introduced in a national context of increasing disunity and discord. As governor, I felt I was trying to counter a process of disintegration, a loosening of social bonds and a growing sense of conflict. This process was marked by a growing feeling of polarity, a feeling of "us" against "them." It was marked by people wanting to take the short view rather than the long view. Often this trend was more a reflection of national life than life in Hawaii, to the extent that one could be distinguished from the other.

My response was to nurture the sense of relatedness and community that I think is one of Hawaii's special strengths. Culturally, this had been taught to me through the word *otagai*, as I have said—the idea of mutual obligation. I think my preoccupation with fair play—dating to my entry into politics in 1954—had a special relevance to the times. People are willing to do their part if they know they are all being treated equally.

From experience I believed government could not be all things and do all things. I refused to pretend that it could. I developed a reputation for looking critically at proposals for new spending. I often said no to people who wanted a yes answer. Politically, I got away with it because people knew I wasn't playing favorites.

At the same time I took many innovative steps in the social and community spheres, and in economic development. I didn't see lean financial times as a reason to stop innovating. On the contrary, the importance of well-planned economic development became more clearly urgent. Some of my Administration's initiatives are working today. Some were ahead of their time. Some were considered a little far out. Some have been undermined, but I believe that most of them will of necessity be revived.

In my approach to the problems of the 1970s, I was never particularly partisan. I tried to heal old wounds and to avoid harsh words.

Today I look back over my Administration mainly for the purpose of speaking authentically about shared concerns which affect us now, and which will affect our future. I am deeply worried about where we are going. My concern is for our entire society, and not my political party *per se*, but I must say to my fellow Democrats that if we are to provide real leadership we must regroup ourselves and refocus our efforts. The political process is bogged down in endless petty details that obscure the needed course of action on the major issues. When I attended the 1994 State Democratic Convention, I heard many words of praise for Governor Burns and myself. While I appreciated these words I was distressed that I heard so little about visions for the future.

Part of the heritage of my parents' generation was embodied in the phrase, *kodomo no tame ni,* "for the sake of the children." My parents' generation had a deep understanding of their responsibility to the future, and we today have an equal responsibility to the future. Not only to be right but to be effective, we must be understanding of the feelings of others and the needs of others in the process. The whole idea of, "Do unto others as you would have them do unto you," is another way of saying *otagai*. It's a way of acknowledging our connection to suffering. It reflects the sense that, "There but for the grace of God go I."

As governor, I wanted every person to be willing to listen to the other person's point of view, not necessarily for the purpose of going along, but to be attuned to a wide range of thought and opinion. If we put all viewpoints on the table, we can learn from them. I was reminded almost daily that some people are vocal, but others are not. You always hear from the people who are loud and speak up. Because of this, political leaders have a responsibility to draw out the views and feelings of the people who are less vocal. This occurs when the principle of *otagai* is practiced, when mutuality is understood and mutual respect is exercised.

The difference between failure and success is not that great. People have similar talents but they have differences in performance. We see this in athletics, when one team is better on some days, and another team is better on others. It's that little bit of difference, that little bit of effort, doing the right things, doing them in the right way, recognizing that you have other people who are involved, trying to be fair, trying to do your best under any circumstances, and knowing it is not only the big things but the little things that count.

Often people in leadership positions feel the need to make ringing pronouncements. The reality is that things get done little by little. A chief executive and his top administrators cannot begin to do all that needs to be done. Accomplishment is built on getting people to give a little extra feeling and thought and make a little extra effort.

You must tell people in the government workforce what has to be done, but you must also help them appreciate why their individual tasks are important. People working at many different things can all fit together, but they need to know why and how. As governor I had the opportunity to spread the message. I tried to visit every department and talk with all the thousands of employees of State government, dividing them into groups as necessary. When I was finished, I repeated the cycle, attempting to complete it every four years. No one was unimportant.

I walked through many government worksites at Christmas and before the New Year, to greet people and chat with them. I hoped to convey that their efforts were appreciated, that I wished them well, and that we had to renew ourselves for the challenges that lay ahead. Such simple things are important.

Instead of hiring more and more people, I preferred having fewer people and expecting more from them. I would tell them, "If you can try hard enough, and produce enough, I don't have to hire all these extra people." I tried to avoid part-time hires and contract hires, a practice that creates separate categories of State employees. I wanted everyone to feel they were in it together. I wanted everyone to work hard and get such benefits as the public could afford. I told government employees that they knew their jobs better than anyone else, that they were the experts, and I was counting on them to share their expertise fully.

In my selection of people to State government boards and commissions, I sought to make them as diverse as possible in geography, interests, and employment, so they represented a broad cross-section of the community. When people were sworn in I told them, "Don't be afraid to speak up because you may have a different idea. That's why you're here." I said I would not come to them to direct their work, or to second-guess their work, and I didn't.[10]

I talked with people throughout the government about not being afraid to make mistakes. I urged people to regard problems as challenges, and they had to take risks to meet those challenges. "If you get too concerned about making a mistake," I said, "you will take the safe course. The safe course is to do today exactly as you did yesterday. It is the tried and safe route. But society does not stand still. Society is constantly evolving. Taking the same course in government year after year means you are standing still, and to stand still is to lose ground, because everything around us is changing."

Therefore it was imperative that people seek out new ways of conducting government and take risks in the process. I said, "You have to be creative. You have to find new ways of looking at things. I don't like mistakes in myself, or other people, and I don't want them to become habit-forming, but I can tolerate mistakes far better than I can tolerate the excessive caution that comes from always playing it safe.

"If you make mistakes," I said, "you will learn from them and you will become better and stronger."

I felt it was my job to encourage people, not to control them. To treat

---

[10]I recall only twice in twelve years that I spoke out on specific issues before boards. One was stating publicly that the Land Use Commission should give a full airing—rather than an abbreviated hearing—to a proposed commuter airport near Lahaina (subsequently located at Kaanapali, Maui). A second time I voiced my opposition to a move in the Nursing Board to require a college degree, which I thought was excessive. I also spoke to the Land Board on the general importance of my new land and water policies.

people with dignity, you have to recognize they are capable of doing things on their own, and you can't control them successfully by treating them like robots. No matter how brilliant a person is, he or she has to depend on others. People must be ready to say, "I have to do my best, because others are counting on me."

In choosing people for jobs, when I gave cabinet positions to supporters of political opponents, they sometimes would say, "Gee, I supported so-and-so." I would say, "That's okay. All I expect is that you do a good job." Many people in the fields of social work and the helping professions had been supporters of Tom Gill. Some of these exemplary individuals became key figures in my Administration.

I tried to spend time with my appointees to convey my philosophy. I outlined what I expected of them. Then I said, "Go to it." While I tried to avoid putting people in impossible situations, I often threw them into challenging situations, believing in their potential. My philosophy was the same as I had watching my children learn to walk. If you are so afraid the baby will fall down, you will not let the baby stand up. As part of its learning process, *the baby has to fall down.*

In staffing the government, I started with what needed to be done, then looked for the best individuals to do it. While this may sound elemental, it is worth thinking about, because the natural temptation is to do the opposite—hire someone you like and then try to figure out what you want them to do.

My feeling about respecting the integrity of relationships led me to a cabinet-oriented approach to governing. I tried to select people who could exercise the responsibility entrusted to them. I gave them limits or constraints, fiscal and otherwise, and set forth broad policies. I then allowed them to perform freely within those guidelines. I put them in charge and let them manage. I did not pull strings, believing it would have been insulting.

One of the important tasks of the cabinet is to work with the Legislature. As a former legislator, I knew how important it is to have all the facts and all the viewpoints. It is then that the best thinking occurs and the best decisions are made. Accordingly I encouraged my cabinet members to give legislators the full benefit of their thinking, even if this led to presenting conflicting views. At one point I was severely criticized for two of my department directors taking conflicting positions before the Legislature. I didn't mind, because I knew that conflicting views result from the fact that cabinet members have different missions. To give but one obvious example, the viewpoint of an administrator of housing programs is far different from one who promotes the diversification of agriculture. Criticism for airing differences publicly was a modest price to pay for giving people autonomy and responsibility.

For a large part of my staff in the governor's office, I chose young, idealistic people who were full of ideas and energy. Because of continuous budget constraints, they worked for modest salaries. Most of them worked such long hours that they joked about working for the minimum wage. I told them, "The future belongs to you more than it belongs to me." I was extremely proud of them.

At some point I would try to have a long conversation with each one. I would say, "I looked back, and I saw you folks coming, and I reached back and grabbed you folks, and I pulled so that you could come up the path. There are many other people coming up the path behind you, so from time to time you have to reach back and help them along." I often talked with them about my concept of *stewardship*. I said it means that you may temporarily have or hold something in the knowledge that it is not yours to keep. It is only yours to use, and you should use it in a way that the next person can come along and use it after you. The next person can pick up where you left off. The next person can likewise be a good steward and practice concern for the next generation. This idea is of the utmost importance. What we have today does not belong to us without qualification. It is ours to care for, enjoy, and make better before passing it on. We are stewards of elective office. We are stewards of jobs, institutions, and communities, just as we are stewards of the land and stewards of all our resources.

THERE IS A QUOTE FROM THE CHINESE PHILOSOPHER Lao Tsu that I like: "A leader is best when the people hardly know he exists. And of that leader the people will say when his work is done, 'We did this ourselves.'" It was used in a film, "Boy From Kalihi," produced for the 1978 campaign on my behalf. Today this quote helps me explain my approach to the role of a governor in public dialogue.

If you tell people to do something, they may actually try to do it, but they will tend to give up easily. If something becomes their idea as well as yours, and if you work on it together, they can't say, "That stupid Ariyoshi, it was his idea. Let's give up." They will say, "I had a part in this. I have to make it work." When you consider that the difference between succeeding and failing is slight, one of the differences can be the extra effort people will give when they feel they are genuinely involved and responsible.

The governor's job is to set a broad general direction and inspire people to believe they can make progress in that direction. People want somebody who can look at the entire community and say what is going well and what needs to be worked on. This overview is the road map. Once people agree on a road map they see a variety of ways to get from one place to the next.

In some instances, the governor needs to help mold and shape public opinion, but again I believe this must be done in a general way. You can get overly specific and end up bickering over the details of policy in the press. That is no way to communicate, because it is fraught with the potential for misunderstanding and polarization.

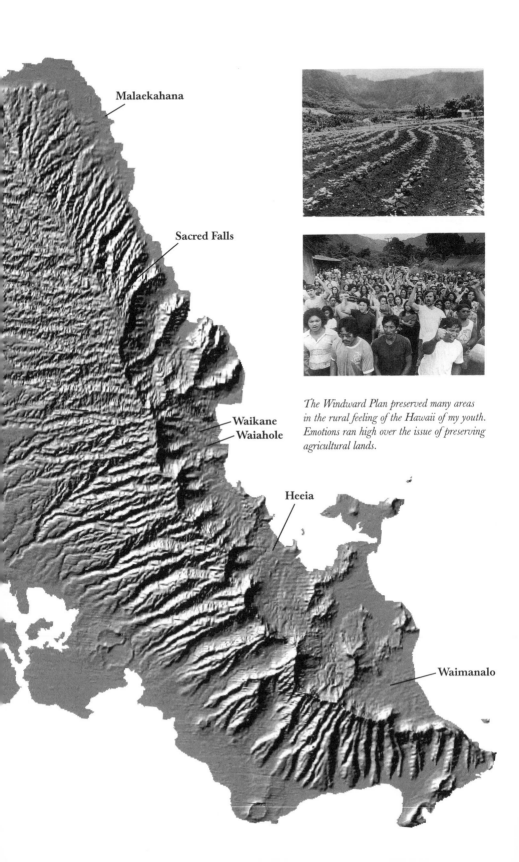

Malaekahana

Sacred Falls

Waikane
Waiahole

Heeia

Waimanalo

The Windward Plan preserved many areas in the rural feeling of the Hawaii of my youth. Emotions ran high over the issue of preserving agricultural lands.

CHAPTER SEVEN

The Issue

WE DEMOCRATS HAD COME INTO OFFICE determined to break up the economic domination of the old Big Five companies which had grown out of the plantation system. To support our plans for a new Hawaii, we not only needed to break up the interlocking directorates but also stimulate real economic growth as well. Economic growth would lead Hawaii to *new* opportunities, and these would give reality to the Democrat Party's promise of *equal* opportunity.

For a long time, events played into our hands. Throughout the 1960s and early 1970s, Hawaii's economy grew rapidly. Statehood attracted investment to Hawaii. It greatly accelerated the growth of tourism. The jet airplane cut travel time to Hawaii to less than half of what it had been. Aircraft were redesigned to carry many more people on a flight. Alongside our traditional agricultural and military sectors, a large service economy grew up. Many new jobs were generated. Where Hawaii had been a near-subsistence economy in ancient Hawaiian times, and then had been a highly controlled economy in plantation times, within just a few years we developed a dynamic economy that was interrelated with the national and global economies.

More and more people streamed into Hawaii. When I became governor, the population of most states was growing at eight-tenths of one percent a year. The population of Hawaii was growing at two and four-tenths percent a year, or three times the national average. Yet another factor was bearing on us heavily. It was the displacement of Southeast Asians resulting from the Vietnam War, causing an in-migration from that region of four times the national average.

We were reeling from the effects of an ever-accelerating population growth. On December 7, 1941, Hawaii had a population of 423,000. By the year of Statehood, 1959, the population was 633,000. By the time I was elected in 1974, it had grown to 868,000. In a brief thirty years, our population had doubled. We had become a fast-growing tourist destination and a fast-growing state. We were an extension of the most powerful nation on earth. We were poised literally halfway out into the Pacific region, which was becoming the most dynamic region of the globe. If this rate of growth were to continue, the economist Thomas Hitch calculated, the Hawaiian Islands of the year 2074 would have fourteen million people.

While so much was changing, one thing could not change. We were still a set of fragile islands. The rapid growth that previously had been thought of as good, and which well may have been thought of as good in other states, was no longer good for our State.

I was convinced that neither our infrastructure nor our environment would support this rate of growth. *At the rate we were growing, we were going to destroy our State.* In our attempts to cope with such a rate of growth, we were concentrating too many resources on creating employment. We were opening up too much land, using too much water, building too much, and taking too many chances with our environment.

As governor, I had to face these trends squarely and try to develop answers. I had to be a new kind of Democrat and a new kind of governor while continuing to draw on the strengths of our tradition and philosophy. In the early phases I was more reactive. I generated or embraced a set of novel and controversial ideas. As time went on, broadly based teams came together. Through these teams we developed new and more complex thinking. We became proactive. We generated prototypes of answers, and then we generalized our prototypes into far-reaching policy and legislation.

Initially our growth problems were brought into focus by in-migration and the rapidly rising cost of our welfare assistance program. I had gone one round with the problem of welfare as lieutenant governor, and I went a second round as governor. What had been a $10 million welfare program in 1960 had become a $64 million welfare program by 1970. As part of our liberal tradition, we policymakers in Hawaii had prided ourselves on taking care of the poor. In the process we had set up the most generous welfare payments in the nation. Our programs were intended for the genuinely needy among us in Hawaii, but increasingly the money went to the voluntary poor who were migrating to our Islands from across the ocean.

The Welfare Office had heard stories of "hippies" on the West Coast creating an old-fashioned picture of paradise. The story, apparently widely repeated among young, experimental Mainlanders, was that Hawaii's weather was ideal, the environment was ideal, and one could live out in the open, on the beaches or in the mountains. Best of all, one could go directly to the Welfare Office and immediately get on welfare.

Worst of all, the story was true. People were arriving at the airport and telling cab drivers, "Take me to the nearest welfare office." One study found that more than half of all applicants for welfare had lived in Hawaii less than one year.

In response to this situation, I urged the Legislature to pass a residency requirement. I was told, "You can't do that, it's unconstitutional," a reference to a 1969 ruling by the U.S. Supreme Court. I said, "I know, but at least we'll serve notice to people that they have to test us—and maybe take us to court." While ultimately our law was ruled unconstitutional, it at least served as a stop-gap measure.

I dug more deeply into a web of related population and growth issues. I had a friend who hired an immigrant for an entry-level job. Practically the next day, the person quit to qualify for welfare assistance. Many of the new immigrants were conscientious workers who wanted to become contributing members of the community. But as a matter of policy, in contrast to the earlier experience of immigrants to America, we were starting people off in a new country by saying, "Get assistance. You don't have to go to work." This was pathetic. We were taking basically hardworking people and teaching them a brand-new cultural idea, "You don't have to work—government will take care of you." That was a terrible message, yet that was our message when people came *en masse* as refugees from the war in Southeast Asia.

By way of contrast, I thought of my parents, and of all the earlier immigrants from Asia and Europe. It is true they had to struggle, but their presence usually had some basis in economics. Unlike these earlier immigrations, the movement of people in the mid-1970s was being orchestrated by the Federal government, which was running a relocation agency at the time. This agency was guiding refugees out of camps in Southeast Asia and Guam into American communities, ours in particular. I strongly expressed my concerns to Federal representatives. I gave them ideas for simultaneously relocating people and finding jobs or training. I told them we simply did not have the infrastructure, employment base, housing, or land that were needed to absorb the refugees in the numbers, and at the pace, being imposed upon us. My position was distorted by critics in such a way that I was portrayed as anti-immigrant. I felt pressed to explain myself to the 1978 convention of the Democratic Party. I said that if the Federal government could regulate the number of immigrants who enter the country, "then the various states must also have some voice in how many can settle in their state."

I pointed out that national quotas are a statement of how many people a nation believes it can satisfactorily absorb at one time, but that states had no such protection. I also made a presentation to a meeting of the National Governors Association on the problems of in-migration and welfare.

I should stress I was not concerned about the kind or quality of the people who were coming. There are many people in Hawaii today who came then and who have worked hard, done well, and made a contribution. My concern was being able to accommodate so many at one time and to assimilate them to become contributing members of society. There were times when my message fell on deaf ears, but I think eventually my voice was heard. The relocation effort began to direct immigrants to areas that traditionally did not have Asian-American populations, and I think everyone benefited.

HAWAII'S WELFARE SYSTEM WAS ORIGINALLY DESIGNED for a stable population that was for the most part eager to work, and now the system was running out of control for reasons that had nothing to do with its origins or our intentions. The challenge was to address problems resulting from voluntary unemployment, but to avoid hurting innocent children in any way—that is, regardless of the status of the parents. In our initial phase we closed loopholes that existed between our welfare and unemployment laws, so that people who either left jobs or were fired for good cause could be denied welfare. After what seemed to be endless rounds of legislative and court battles, I got a second law through the 1978 Legislature. It said that able-bodied people under fifty-five years of age without dependents could not receive a category of aid known as General Assistance, which was one hundred percent funded by the State government. I should stress this in no way affected the Aid to Families with Dependent Children program, which does what its name states. The restrictions affected able-bodied local people under age fifty-five as well as those coming from the airport, which meant this new law *was* constitutional.

I was comfortable with applying this standard to residents as well as newcomers. General Assistance to able-bodied people of working age fostered dependence and made people weaker. It made people dependent on the system rather than forcing them to provide for themselves.

I FOUGHT RELATED BATTLES in which I attempted to impose residency requirements on State jobs. I even raised the issue of a constitutional amendment to restrict immigration from abroad. When I talked about the need for us in Hawaii to have some control over our population's growth, a lot of people told me that I was being un-American. I told them, "I know it may seem that way, but if we keep growing at the present rate we won't be able to handle all the people who will come." If I can put my finger on one thing that generated support for this effort, it was that people felt I was more concerned about the long term than the short term. I encouraged a lot of people to participate and try things that would move us in the right direction.

BENEATH THE POPULATION ISSUE lay the issues of land and water. How were the land and water resources of Hawaii to be used? What quality of life was to result? And—as we worked, the question evolved—how could land and water be managed to influence patterns of population growth?

By definition, land and water are limited throughout the globe, but perhaps nowhere is this fact so clearly perceived as in the precious, fragile island environment of Hawaii. Hawaii is so beautiful and so much in demand. It is a full participant in the largest and most technologically advanced economy on earth, that of the United States. It is significantly influenced by the second largest national economy, Japan. While there are island nations such as Japan, the United Kingdom, and the Philippines, their land masses are so large that we do not usually think of them in the genre of islands. By contrast, the city of Honolulu is a big urban center on a truly small island. Between North America and New Zealand, Honolulu is, by far, the largest tropical island city. The population of the State of Hawaii exceeds that of many independent nations in the Pacific. In this part of the globe, only the nation of Fiji is comparable in scale to Hawaii; but even Fiji has fewer people and more land than does Hawaii.

In the early Statehood period, we celebrated the fact that we were finally a state of the United States. In my time as governor, people began to focus increasingly on the fact that Hawaii is America's only *island* state. We began to work seriously with the fact that the amount of land we urbanized, and the amount of water supplied to it, could be an effective and constitutional control on population growth.

We worked on several issues more or less simultaneously. One was an immediate conflict over the proposed urbanization of the Waiahole-Waikane farming community, which is in a beautiful pair of interrelated valleys on the windward side of Oahu. The second effort, which evolved in parallel, was development of a regional plan for Windward Oahu.

The third related task was a general plan of unprecedented depth and breadth—a general plan for the entire State of Hawaii.

The planning issues posed by Windward Oahu would turn out to be pivotal. I asked myself, and I asked others, "What can we do to help preserve a part of old Hawaii—the Hawaii that we knew as youngsters? Does it still exist in some places? Is there a chance we can save some of that? Can we enable our grandchildren to experience the environment of old Hawaii that we experienced?" The windward side of Oahu was the most likely next step in the rapid process of urbanization, so the easy answer was to fall back on the Neighbor Islands. But I agreed with the many people who were determined that we not let Windward Oahu be overrun by urbanization, because the Windward Oahu that lay past the town of Kaneohe was still much like the Hawaii of old. We had the opportunity for it to remain relatively undeveloped, to be rural and agricultural in nature.

As events unfolded, the plan for Windward Oahu loomed as a vivid reminder that we either had to take control of growth or growth would take control of us. The valleys of Waiahole and Waikane were the next readily accessible valleys up the windward coast, so they lay most directly in the path of urbanization. The land was owned by the McCandless Estate. It was the site of traditional small farming. The leases were month to month, and the infrastructure for agriculture was inadequate, which tended to discourage proper planning and investment. The resulting income to the McCandless Estate was relatively low, and the heir, Mrs. Elizabeth McCandless Marks, was looking to do something more with the land. Before Waiahole-Waikane became much of an issue, she was far along in her negotiations with a well-known developer. Plans were announced that Waiahole-Waikane would become an enormous subdivision, with more than seven thousand homes to be built over a period of ten years.

The farming community felt threatened, and indeed it *was*. Farmers were sent new leases, which sometimes quadrupled their lease rents. When they refused to pay they were given eviction notices. The farmers' cause became the cause of activists who proliferated in the 1970s as a manifestation of vast social unrest. On the fringe, some individuals were talking about violence. A few were enthralled with the idea of violent revolution and the establishment of a new order.

We had long, frustrating meetings. I was the object of political harangues and personal attacks on my motives and integrity. I tried to take these in stride, but a point came at which I did not. It was the one time I remember displaying my anger. I threw my papers on the table and said, "If you read these, you will know I am trying to help you people." I left.

The more I studied the situation the more I became determined to use the Waiahole-Waikane conflict to advance the cause of planning and preservation.

I entered into a negotiation with Mrs. Marks and her attorney. I invited them to Washington Place and talked with them repeatedly, face to face. I told Mrs. Marks how important the property was to the windward side. I told her how she could be a participant in preserving an earlier-day Hawaii. I suggested that if she sold the land, she would have the money to use as she saw fit, free of the public debate in which she had become enmeshed. I said I would be extremely grateful to her if she would agree to the sale of the property. We talked off and on for several days. Finally she agreed to sell the six hundred acres of the valley for $6 million. At the time I thought of it as a low price—thanks in part to her desire to be public-spirited—and today it seems like a pittance to pay for the best land, and all the water to go with it, in an entire, beautiful valley of Oahu. I think it was the best $6 million the State government ever spent.

At the moment, there was little praise and lots of criticism. We concluded our negotiations on a Saturday morning. Almost immediately I made a brief announcement and left for a necessary, scheduled trip to Washington. By the time I got to Washington, the telephone lines were buzzing. My staff was getting a barrage of angry calls. Legislators were contending that the State government merely had acquired the landowner's and developer's problems, and that we now would have to deal directly with a lot of fiercely independent tenant farmers and their angry supporters as well. My response was to let the controversy simmer for a couple of days. I said, "When I get home I'll explain why I did this, and it will be okay." Some influential legislators threatened to not provide the funds, but I was able to use funds that were already available.

In this heated political environment my Administration turned to the broader task of formulating the Windward Regional Plan. I brought a team together that worked long and hard on looking at facts in new ways and generating new ideas. The Windward Oahu Plan created a framework of new processes and principles. It included systematic input through survey research from the general public. I saw this as giving voice to that huge majority of community members who usually don't have an opportunity to get their opinions across.

The Windward Plan was an early draft of the idea of growth management, which was to evolve as the most important concept of my twelve-year elected Administration. The Windward Plan outlined options for managing population growth, and it generated new thinking on the available legal means of managing growth. It explored the pressure of urbanization, the desire for expanding suburban areas, and also what was needed to maintain rural, agricultural, and conservation areas. Obviously our emphasis was on the latter. The Windward Plan was governmental homework. It created a rational framework for slowing down physical development and population growth and maintaining the rural character of the region.

Our planning approach was faithful to the traditional importance of geographic districts that had been handed down to us from ancient times. We did not know it at the time, but recent research is pointing to Windward Oahu as the site of the first extensive human settlement by Hawaiians—which is yet another reason to preserve a sense of old Hawaii in that area. The Plan stimulated other regions to pursue consensus planning as a way of achieving their goals—which typically had to do with slowing down growth, preserving agriculture, and taking care of our unique environment.

The Windward Plan had a far-reaching impact which, I hope, will prove to be timeless. Today you can see the effect when you drive out along the windward shore of Oahu. I personally am thrilled by it, because I get back in touch with the Hawaii of my childhood. I imagine how my grandson, Sky, will experience the Hawaii I knew during my years in the little community of Laie. I certainly did not generate all the feelings that went into the Windward Plan, but I shared those feelings. I focused them as the priority work of the top policymakers in the State government of Hawaii.

The Windward Plan created a rational basis for ideas and feelings that otherwise were fragments floating in the air. The plan allowed us to proceed with an aggressive program of growth management that might otherwise have been undermined by parochial legislative and political interests.

LAND BANKING TO PRESERVE KEY AREAS of Windward Oahu caused an intense debate within the Administration. In reality this was a debate over the long-term good to be derived from the Windward Plan versus the short-term popularity of my Administration. The question was whether to buy more properties, as we had bought Waiahole Valley, and preserve them (or "land bank" them), even if the properties weren't put to agricultural or park use within the life of my Administration. Should we buy as much land as we could for posterity? Or should we buy only as much land as we could quickly press into public use and get credit for in the next election?

Advisors who took the near-term view told me I should *not* spend more money on land banking. Rather, I should spend money developing parks and farmlands. If we didn't put the money into high-visibility projects, how would the voting public know what we were doing?

I used that occasion to tell our people, "The best political strategy is to do what is right, and let that speak for us. If we try to always put short-term political thinking into the equation, the equation is going to be skewed, and we won't come out with the best decisions." If we lost opportunities to preserve part of old Hawaii, I would not be able to hold my head up. I would not feel good about what we did, and I would not be able to ask people—with an inner clarity and clear conscience—for their political support.

With that as our guide, we pursued conservation to the maximum— moving urgently to stay ahead of the plans of land developers. In a short period, proposals were advanced for new resorts, shopping centers, golf courses, and many thousands of houses. In their cumulative effect, these proposals would have thoroughly urbanized Windward Oahu. A proposal arose to develop tourism at Heeia Kea, which is a picturesque site accented by an enormous coastal Hawaiian fishpond from ancient times. I was dead set against this development plan. I felt tourism should be confined to a few carefully planned sites, principally Waikiki. Most visitors seem to enjoy the bright lights of Kalakaua Avenue, but when they get out in the country they want to see tropical Hawaii. We definitely should not have resort facilities spread out over the island. We bought the site at Heeia Kea and protected it.

Further upcountry, along the Windward coast, I looked at Malaekahana Bay. I thought it would make a beautiful park. Some people in the neighborhood didn't want the State to buy the bay area because they feared a park would bring people in from other parts of the island—in their minds, "from the outside." I told them, "This is one community, one state. People are coming anyway, so you might as well control the circumstances by making a park." We bought Malaekahana and preserved it from development. Today Malaekahana is a wonderful retreat from urban and suburban life.

Beyond Waiahole Valley, past the pleasant turn of Kahana Bay, is a special upland site called Sacred Falls. In competition with a developer's elaborate plan, we bought over fourteen hundred acres. These acres are to be preserved in perpetuity from development. Similarly, beyond Kahuku Point on the North Shore, an influential developer had filed a subdivision plan for Kaiaka Point in the Waialua-Haleiwa area. I particularly remember an eloquent plea from a woman who was a long-time resident, Marguerite "Peggy" Paty. She said it would be criminal to allow the development to preempt the enjoyment of future generations. We stepped in and bought the entire point of land overlooking the coastline, and today it too is a park. We bought other small, strategically located properties up and down the coast in conjunction with the City government, always with the goal of maintaining the rural character of Oahu in the face of urbanization. The opportunities to preserve the land in perpetuity were there, and I believed I had an obligation to future generations.

Although the character of Oahu was most at issue, the idea of preserving special places was not confined to our most densely populated island. One of the most notable examples of preservation occurred at a beautiful ocean-front place on southeast Kauai called Kipukai. Kipukai is a half-moon bay with a series of beaches, surrounded by ridges not only on the sides but in the back as well. The result is a separate, cloistered world of over a thousand acres, which has been little changed by the hands of humans. While I was on the board of First Hawaiian Bank I sometimes would sit next to a fellow director, Jack Waterhouse, who owned Kipukai. Jack Waterhouse originally had ridden a horse down the ridgeline into Kipukai. He built a simple road and was engaged in weekend ranching. After I became so involved as governor in conserving open space, he and I revived our conversation about the place. I visited Kipukai and wrote a note in the guestbook that it was "a treasure worth preserving for generations to come." Subsequently he deeded the land to the State of Hawaii with the provision that it be used as a natural preserve. The State is to take possession when the last of his nieces and nephews are gone, and it will cost the public nothing.

CHAPTER EIGHT

The Hawaii State Plan

As we worked on the many problems associated with rapid growth, various pieces began to merge into a unique, unprecedented policy. It was a selective growth policy, or a growth management policy. In my speeches, I often talked about our "preferred future," because I wanted to constantly remind people that the core of our selective growth policy was making the right choices about our future.

I sensed people gaining a broader perspective. After the intense physical changes that had been occurring in Hawaii, I think it was partly a matter of recovering a sense of balance. People began to more readily say, "Let's make the decisions that will have the greatest positive impact on the future."

One of the most important elements of this emerging policy was support for diversified agriculture. In addition to the sugar and pineapple plantations that originally developed the modern economy of the Islands, Hawaii has a potential to further expand in the growing of fruit, vegetables, nuts, flowers, ornamental plants and foliage, as well as other forms of diversified agriculture. But when I took over the governorship, diversified agriculture was in decline. I was determined to reverse this process and set diversified agriculture on a new, more productive path. Perhaps because people were so used to our landscape being incrementally urbanized, my call for the revival and diversification of agriculture was met with a great deal of skepticism. I remember in particular a speech I gave to the Chamber of Commerce. It was received as if I had embraced a remote dream.

Nonetheless, to be serious about maintaining the lifestyle and environment we so valued, we had to make open space productive. Again, Windward Oahu was the setting for bringing the issue of agriculture into focus. During the 1957 Legislature, when we were still a Territory, a group of farmers came lobbying for the government to sell them the land they were farming. This land was situated in the beautiful community of Waimanalo, on the far eastern part of Windward Oahu, just around the coastline from the growing suburbs of Hawaii Kai.

The land was sold to the farmers at farmland prices, with a restrictive covenant that the land be used for agriculture for at least twenty years. The farmers said, "Sure, no problem. We're farming anyway." But with the passage of time they approached the end of their farming days, and many of their children weren't interested in farming. As the end of the twenty-year restriction approached in 1977, during my first term, they were talking about wanting to get their property zoned for urban use.

I saw what a short time twenty years is in the life of a community. I thought to myself, "If we're going to have agriculture as a permanent part of our future, we have to determine the use of the land in perpetuity." If government land was sold off to private owners in fee simple, we would have difficulty keeping land in agriculture. Owners would be continuously generating schemes for urbanization, addressing needs for housing, or economic development, or places to shop, and at the right moment some of the land would be rezoned. I saw very clearly that while zoning is one form of protecting land for a certain use, zoning is not enough. As an alternative, I turned to a concept of creating agricultural preserves, or "parks."

We started with State land. The idea was to have readily arable land that farmers could actually afford to lease, because it doesn't help to zone land for agriculture and then tell the farmer, "We're charging you ten thousand dollars an acre for the use of it." We put in water and simple roads for access. We then put the resulting "agricultural park" out for use. We told people, "You don't have to bid for this property, but you draw lots for it. You can farm this property at agricultural rates. You can have this land as long as you use it for farming, and you can develop a good business and pass the land on to your children so long as they also want to use the land in the same way." People could either farm full-time or part-time, but as long as they kept the land productive they could have long-term leases. While agricultural parks are not what people think of as land development, they are in fact a form of development.

Fairly quickly, we opened up agricultural parks all over the State.

As I promoted the "ag" parks, I found there were a lot of people going to the University of Hawaii School of Agriculture who wanted land to farm. I wanted to help them because I thought they would make an invaluable contribution to the community. I think of farmers as a special breed. They get up early and live with the fluctuations of the weather. They experience adversity. They get flooded, they get wiped out, and they come back. They plant again. In the history of our country, the farmer has played a vital role. It's important that our communities have people with that kind of toughness.

Agricultural parks also are a way to keep Hawaii green. They keep open space productive. Productivity creates jobs and contributes to the tax base. Productivity also guarantees that real people with a direct self-interest will stand up to defend open space against development. Society has a hard time going against the direct interests of its farmers.

Diversified agriculture beautifies our landscape and helps create an interesting experience for visitors. It also helps Hawaii's consumers, who all too often spend their money on food that is inflated by the cost of importation. A thriving local farm business produces food that is fresher, better, and healthier. During my tenure, a $35 million industry in "other crops" (meaning they were neither sugar nor pineapple) grew to nearly $148 million. The livestock industry grew from $58 million to $83 million. Today the upward trend of diversified crops continues. Of even greater importance is the base that has been laid for diversified agriculture now that the demise of sugar and pineapple plantations is freeing up large amounts of land and water.

Much of my drive to diversify agriculture had to do with small farmers, but I encouraged interested corporations to get involved as well. At one of my talks I noticed a cheerful-looking fellow listening intently to every word. Soon thereafter John "Doc" Buyers of C. Brewer and Co. was in my office. He said, "I liked what you said. I wanted to talk with you, because I have some thoughts about agriculture too." He talked about the Kilauea area of Kauai, which is on the road to the North Shore. C. Brewer originally had a plantation in Kilauea. Some of the land was sold, then it was sold again, appreciating many times over. If land was going to go up so much in price it eventually would be taken out of agricultural zoning and be put to uses that would not be good for Kauai. I felt we ought not to encourage industrial and urban uses but keep the Kilauea area in agricultural production to the maximum extent possible. "Doc" Buyers and I developed a plan to subdivide the land for agricultural purposes, and to create a legal covenant "to run with the land," which became part of the land deed. The subsequent owners would be bound by the covenant, which provided that the land could only be taken out of agriculture at the government's initiative, guaranteeing the land would always be sold at agricultural values. Because "Doc" Buyers was far-sighted about agriculture, he agreed to do this without any compensation to his company.

Joanne Yukimura, an environmental activist, was on the Kauai County

Council when this idea emerged. She came to me and asked, "Will this really keep the land in agriculture?" I said, "Find me a better set of guarantees if you can, but this set of guarantees lies not only in agricultural zoning but is written directly into the covenant." And, I added, "We're not paying one cent for it." Years later when Joanne became mayor she praised the way the land not only was in agriculture but was commercially viable as well.

"Doc" Buyers has been responsible for planting thousands of trees in Hawaii. To me this reflects a corporate commitment to the long-term future of our island State. When "Doc" was struggling with the problem of fueling an electrical generator, he set out to find a constant source of re-supply. Research led him to the eucalyptus tree, which is full of resin and grows a foot a month. In five years it will grow to be sixty feet tall. You can cut off fifty feet for fuel and leave a ten-foot stump, and it will grow again and again. He and I planted thousands of eucalyptus trees.

He also was looking ahead for alternative crops that would be in great demand. He settled on macadamia nuts, even though a macadamia nut tree takes seven years to mature and bear fruit. He planted hundreds of acres of macadamia and now the nuts are being harvested, providing revenue to his company.

When I went to the dedication of the agricultural land at Kilauea, Kauai, I planted a guava tree. Previously guava had been picked unevenly in the wild, but this tree became part of a large orchard of a new hybrid of guava developed by the University of Hawaii. When I see "Doc" I ask him, "How is that tree coming along?" "Doc" tells me, "If we let any tree die, it's not going to be that tree."

The message of ecology is that "everything is related to everything." The message of being governor of the island state of Hawaii is much the same. When you sit in the Legislature, you can study an issue and become an advocate of a particular viewpoint. When you sit in the chair of the governor, you must look at a web of things. You must discern patterns, and then decide whether to try to move the community in a certain direction.

You cannot think about land issues without thinking about water issues; conservation of water is inseparable from conservation of the land. The most dramatic example of our watershed is Mount Waialeale on Kauai, which has over five hundred inches of rainfall a year, more than any other place on earth. The heart of Kahana Valley on Oahu is also one of the wettest places in the world, and generally the mountainous areas of our Islands are invaluable as sources of recharging our underground water system.

My Administration thought a lot about water issues and made some far-reaching changes in water management. I want to tell you why, because water is one of those subjects that becomes more important with each passing day. As governor, I faced constant demands to streamline the land-permit process in the name of attracting capital and developing the economy. I always took the position you can streamline the permit system up to a point, but you should never eliminate the State Land Use Commission, which is unique in the nation as a statewide land-zoning agency. The Land Use Commission plays a vital role in defining and protecting conservation lands. If land is ever taken out of conservation, nature's capacity to replenish the supply of water decreases while demand for the use of water increases.

The urbanization of land requires enormous amounts of water. Farming is highly water-intensive as well. The supply of water is an important concern throughout most of the State, and over the long run water probably will be the single most important determinant of the carrying capacity of the Hawaiian Islands.

The history of water usage resulted in fragmented management of water. The plantations developed their own water systems, and towns and cities grew up with their own systems. Oahu is a particularly vivid example. All town and city usage was consolidated in the Honolulu Board of Water Supply in 1929, yet each of the plantations had its own system, and military installations had their own systems as well. Nonetheless all were pumping water from what is in the most crucial respect the same source—a great underground reservoir, called a lens, of fresh water.

Briefly and simply stated, this lens of fresh water occurs both above and below sea level in a ratio of one foot of fresh water above sea level to every forty feet of fresh water below sea level. All of this fresh water "floats" on the slightly heavier salt water of the sea, which tends to percolate into the subsurface depths.

Over time, the water table of Oahu had fallen substantially. As I studied our water situation as governor, I came to believe the water table had fallen alarmingly. I became determined to get ahold of the water-management situation. I welcomed and endorsed ratification of a 1978 amendment to the Hawaii Constitution that reads as follows: "The State has an obligation to protect, control, and regulate the use of Hawaii's water resources for the benefit of the people." For my second term in office I assigned water to one of my most trusted staff people, Susumu "Sus" Ono. Sus had been administrative director during my first term, which is comparable to a chief of staff, and in my second term I assigned "Sus" to take over the State Department of Land and Natural Resources and lead the development of a water code.

The result was a conservation-conscious plan that distributed the available supply to urban, industrial, and agricultural uses.

The City and County of Honolulu came to me asking for permission to pump an additional ten million gallons a day. Thinking about the decline in the water table, and the fact that forty feet of water is below sea level for every foot of water above sea level, I challenged them to prove that their request would not damage the water lens. I did not hear from them again, and I never approved their request.

In addition to the underground lens, we looked at surface water, because about one third of the rainfall runs from streams into the sea. We considered damming streams, but people were afraid of dams. We decided we wouldn't try to push that particular idea at the time, but I still think at some point the damming of surface water runoff is going to become important. We will have to figure out how to use it. When we do that we can generate power by hydroelectric means. We also will be able to regulate the flow of water in the streams, which will keep them at an optimal level, healthy and beautiful.

IN ANY ATTEMPT TO ACHIEVE BALANCED GROWTH and meet people's needs, adequate housing emerges as one of society's most difficult problems. The development of housing often conflicts with agriculture. It creates huge demands on the water supply. Furthermore, there is a constant issue of nurturing the dynamics of a free market while guiding physical growth and providing adequate low- and moderate-income housing. When you talk about housing, the question really is, housing for whom?

People often want their own free-standing, single-family houses and their own yards. It is an understandable craving that has resulted in sprawling suburbanization, the destruction of agricultural land, and demand for infrastructure that is often inefficient, or used inefficiently. One of the simplest examples is the way new neighborhoods create demand for new schools, which swell beyond capacity, and then shrink, often below capacity, as the people in the neighborhood grow older.

My administration tried to use marginal lands for housing. That meant avoiding prime agricultural land and also avoiding natural water recharge areas. I encouraged the development of housing in clusters, which ate up less land. Within our resources, I supported the creation of affordable housing by controlling the land, helping with infrastructure, organizing financing, and keeping developer profits at modest levels, reflecting the fact that State government participation had removed most of the risk. The effect of these measures is for society to subsidize housing in a broad, general way, based on a broad social policy goal. As I went forward with my plans for controlled, balanced growth, I was criticized for not opening up huge tracts for the construction of housing, but in fact housing development was always integral to my thinking.

YOU CAN SEE THESE SUBJECTS are not what usually makes for headlines and sound bites. Perhaps they're not as interesting as stories of political conflict, but I hope they're interesting nonetheless, because they will determine the future quality of our society. Politically I sometimes felt I was walking a sort of tightrope by paying so much attention to issues that tended to bear more on the long-term future. I was constantly being criticized by individuals who wanted to sit where I sat. After 1974, the repository of people's dissatisfaction became, almost exclusively for a time, Frank F. Fasi. Fasi had been elected mayor of Honolulu in 1968 and had run unsuccessfully for governor in 1974. Before being elected mayor he had run for a variety of offices and lost,[11] so it was obvious that one loss in a gubernatorial race would not deter him. He was tough, determined, media-smart, and not afraid to take a position. In the making of headlines, I was no match for Frank, and some of the political analysts portrayed me as plodding along toward an almost certain defeat in the 1978 election.

I also was constantly confronted by demonstrations and narrowly focused demands. This was the early stage of what today is widely recognized as single-issue politics. We had protests all the time. There was often a harsh quality to people's anger, which originated from the experience of the war in Vietnam. People became very unhappy with a war that seemed as if it would never end, so they protested. Once they tried it, protests spread to many other areas as well, until mass protest became a way of life. Many times the entire State Capitol would be filled with protesters. Protesters would haunt all the offices, starting with my office

---

[11]Between 1952 and 1968, he won office twice—a one-year term in the Territorial Senate (1958) and a four-year term on the Honolulu City Council (1964-1968). He also served in the 1968 Constitutional Convention.

on the fifth floor, and fill the halls of the other floors, and the courtyard and the steps of the Capitol as well.

I felt Jack Burns was lucky because when people disagreed during his time, they did not disagree that vehemently. But during my time, the questioning of leadership—the confrontation of authority—became the way many people did things. Merely speaking up became an end in itself. If protest was idealistic and hopeful in the 1960s, it often was despairing and hateful in the 1970s.

Once I was going to take a trip to Waiahole. The people responsible for my security insisted that I not go. I said I thought it was important, but they said I would be endangering not only myself but others who went with me. A large element of the people in the demonstration were primarily—and sincerely—concerned about Waiahole. Another element was anti-democratic and antagonistic to the interests of America. They were seeking to capitalize on people's discontent, and they were talking about overthrowing the government. On that one occasion I yielded to the security people, because I agreed we were teetering on the edge of violence.

However, I usually felt an obligation to grasp the viewpoints being expressed in demonstrations, regardless of their tone or tactic. I would try to take the concerns into account in the process of arriving at decisions. Sometimes these were environmental concerns that needed exposure. The early concerns of the native Hawaiian political movement also emerged in demonstrations, and this movement was to have a huge impact on life in Hawaii.

DURING THE TIME I WAS ATTEMPTING TO GENERATE long-term answers to resource issues, the day-to-day economy of Hawaii was in the doldrums. The rate of unemployment was too high, and tax revenues were too low. Again, I should say that the performance of the economy, unemployment, and less-than-satisfactory tax yields are likely to be familiar, recurring problems as time goes on. We escaped these problems in the 1980s as a result of a false prosperity based on massive Federal borrowing (as well as massive corporate and consumer borrowing). But difficult economic times have recurred in the 1990s. It is a cycle we will successfully endure only to experience again. Therefore we must develop a stronger, more conscious philosophy of how to deal with it.

The quick political solution for economic problems is to spend money. It is to turn one's back on what is fiscally sound, issue contracts for construction, consulting, etc., and to generate almost any kind of economic activity. Another aspect of the quick fix is to generate investment in new undertakings, even if it means turning a blind eye to the negative environmental impact. The policy of managed growth was anything but a quick fix. It was unique in the history of Hawaii. It was unique at the state level within the United States and, perhaps, even unique in the context of the developed world. The preeminent importance I assigned to managed growth was not continued when I left office—perhaps understandably. Nonetheless, managed growth will, I believe, only become more important as the years go on. Opportunistic politicians may hide from the need for it, but thoughtful and caring ones will not.

As early as 1974 I made speeches on slowing down Hawaii's rate of growth. These speeches made headlines, so the voting public was advised of my evolving attitude well before I was elected governor. In a larger sense, I probably surprised people. I took a position that few people expected me to take. From 1954 on, I had been consciously dedicated to expanding the economy to create new opportunities. The economic pie had to get bigger. I had agreed to become the first AJA director of First Hawaiian Bank and Honolulu Gas Co. I also had become the first AJA director of Hawaiian Insurance and Guaranty Co., a subsidiary of C. Brewer and Co. As such, I was one of a relatively few Democrats with highly visible ties to business. The slowing of economic growth was more what people might have expected from a Tom Gill, whose criticism of excessive development had become well-known. But the fact was that Tom and I shared a number of the same concerns.

Earlier I traced the experiences as governor that led me to feel that the rapid rate of economic growth would be our undoing. By the summer of 1977, I was ready to generate a comprehensive framework for managing growth. I assembled working task forces to address this concern. I should clarify that I was not seeking a zero-growth policy. With the increases in population, we had to have some economic growth to support it, but I sought to intervene in a spiral of accelerating growth that seemingly was out of control. I sought to foster growth we could accommodate in a healthy way.

That meant growth had to be the right kind, in the right place, at the right pace. It is natural and required of us that we plan. We have the experience of the past and the knowledge of the present as our tools, and we have our obligation as stewards.

I took the resulting ideas of my task force to the 1978 Legislature as the Hawaii State Plan. In my State of the State address, I told how I had urged my policy team "to let their minds run free, not to be constrained by the negative thinkers or by past defeats, and to identify for us possible strategies by which we might reasonably expect to gain some control over our future."

I said the underlying issue was whether "we have the spiritual determination to be masters of our destiny." If we did not seize the opportunity to act, we would look back from the year 2000 on "what might have been." I specifically challenged legislators to take action despite the fact there was an upcoming election.

The State Plan reiterated some of the most basic principles of our society. It spelled out goals and objectives. It included statements of "priority directions" when goals came into conflict. In such areas as housing, transportation, tourism, and agriculture, the State Plan called for the creation of detailed plans. These were referred to as "functional plans," and eventually there were twelve in all.

The State Plan was enacted by that same 1978 session of the Legislature. What the State Plan attempted to do, and what it did, might well be debated. While I was governor the State Plan played an important role. It announced to everyone what the government of Hawaii was seeking to do. It helped unify, coordinate, and rationalize policies. It helped people in government move in the same direction and to recognize cross-purposes from a distance, rather than falling over them. To people who wanted to invest in Hawaii, it served notice of our high standards. It encouraged investment in high-quality, long-range ideas.

We involved all the different people and interests of our diverse community in the State Plan. We went beyond the usual public meetings to public workshops and conferences. We really got people to work. Participants started to think more about the future. As participants were exposed to one another's ideas, they became better citizens with broadened points of view, more able to help guide the development of the future. Through this intensive participatory process, hundreds of people worked on each of the functional plans. They became the greatest proponents of the plans, and they went to the Legislature as citizen-lobbyists and testified effectively for the adoption of the functional plans.

We have many people still active in the community who learned a lot from this process. Some of these people are thought to be opinion leaders. Others are "ordinary voters" who are not really ordinary at all. When you actually listen carefully to people, you're reminded that everyone has something valuable to say.

Part of the State Plan statute called for periodic revision of the plan, which we did. You do not develop plans just for the sake of saying you did so. If a plan is really to be used over time, it must not be set in concrete. You have to ask, "Where are we now? Where is the community? What knowledge do we have about the world?" Good plans are constantly modified.

While I was governor I held up the State Plan and the supporting functional plans to all the State agencies. I said, "When you develop your policies and budgets, ask yourself if you're being consistent with the State Plan. You may not be able to adhere totally to the State Plan, but you have to look at least five and ten years down the road and think about what kind of impact you will have on the future." My administrators got used to doing just that, and for us the State Plan was a vibrant, dynamic tool. With the gentlest of pressure, yet in law, it brought State, County, and private-sector leaders together constantly to work on challenges that had to be dealt with collectively. It encouraged consensus.

Best of all, the State Plan actually helped us manage growth. While it is hard to attribute the slow-down of population growth to any one thing, the State Plan deserves credit in that regard. Where growth had been an unwieldy, destructive two and four-tenths percent per year when I came into office, it was one and seven-tenths percent over my term in office. By 1986, my last year in office, it was less than one and two-tenths percent, or half of what it had been when I came into office.

THE STATE PLAN HAD ITS CRITICS. The upper layers of the Plan were criticized as motherhood and apple pie items, while the functional plans were criticized as being too detailed. The Plan was criticized as being too cumbersome, and for being a collection of good thoughts that often conflicted.

A lack of perfection was inevitable. The State Plan had no precedent. It was hard for people to look at so many things at once. In that sense, we almost need to take a fundamental, evolutionary step as people. We must learn to look at highly complex patterns, conflicting goals, and conflicting priorities in a process of building consensus. The State Plan challenges us to take the message of ecology seriously, and to see what a governor of the Hawaiian Islands sees—that all things are intertwined.

MINI OTEC

(Preceding pages) The deep-ocean pipe at Keahole, Hawaii, brings cold water to the warm Hawaii sun. OTEC is, in my opinion, one of our most exciting alternative energy options.

(Above) Aquaculture and diversified agriculture were high priorities of my Administration. These productive uses are a better guarantee than mere zoning that land will remain in open space, with its rural character maintained.

CHAPTER NINE

Hawaii's Economy

GOVERNORS GET A LOT OF ADVICE. Sometimes people would begin speaking to me by saying, "Back where I came from ... " Occasionally I would respond by saying, "Hawaii is different from 'where you came from.'" While people come to Hawaii looking for something special, inevitably they arrive with their expectations formed by their experiences elsewhere. Most people live on continents, and most Americans live on a huge continent made up of contiguous states. They have massive resources, which are often mined or pumped from the earth. They have heavy industry and access to enormous markets.

Hawaii has none of these. Furthermore, vast stretches of ocean separate us from the large land masses on both sides of us. Shipping products to market is a serious added cost, which makes our products less competitive and sometimes uncompetitive. On the positive side, we have a wonderful environment and a global location that is excellent for learning and experimentation. We have a multicultural people who have been brought together through a uniquely American experience. We have a virtually limitless potential in the creation of services. We have a significant capability in agriculture.

In the realm of economic development, these facts led me away from ideas that either were potentially bad for us, or unrealistic, or both (ideas which typically had to do with the manufacture of products). They led me into areas that were compatible with our long-term well-being.

Governor Burns had illustrated some excellent ways of putting Hawaii's unique attributes to work. The East-West Center on Oahu brings people together for research and study. The astronomy center on top of Mauna Kea on the Big Island is another good example. Mauna Kea is over 14,000 feet in altitude. The atmosphere becomes much thinner at that level, and the air is naturally dry most of the time. Artificial light (which competes with the light to be studied from the universe) is nil on the remote mountain top, and pollution is nonexistent. Governor Burns perceived that astronomy is one of Hawaii's natural industries, as is East-West education.

My experience with the energy crisis suggested to me that development of alternate energy sources could become an industry in itself.
The earth's people are rapidly burning up the readily available supply of
fossil fuels. For our children, or certainly our grandchildren, to continue
to live the lifestyle we've come to expect, we need to develop alternate
sources that are renewable. Hawaii especially needs to do this because
we are almost exclusively dependent on imported oil. Accordingly it
struck me that we could become a global center for researching and
developing new energy sources while lessening our dependence on the
foreign import of oil.

I pushed this idea on the home front in Hawaii, and I pushed it in
Washington as well. At that time the functions of planning and economic
development were in a single department by that name, the Department
of Planning and Economic Development (DPED). I set DPED to work
on the question, and we rapidly identified a range of possibilities. For
decentralized consumer purposes, solar energy had great applicability in
sunny Hawaii. Generators fueled by fast-growing trees (such as eucalyptus) and grasses (such as sugar cane) have a role in the equation. Geothermal from the active volcanoes of the Big Island is potentially a major
source of energy. Yet another source is to be developed by realizing the
ocean's surface is an enormous collector of solar energy.

When Democrat Jimmy Carter was elected president in 1976, two
years after I was elected governor, he created the U.S. Department of
Energy. I spent a lot of time in Washington trying to have them understand us. I was sure by then that we had many resources in Hawaii, and
the challenge was to find the ones that would result in the lowest cost to
consumers. One low-cost way to stretch our resources is to educate people to conserve. We did a lot of that. Through education, coupled with
tax credits, we stimulated the widespread adoption of solar heaters. We
also researched and test-drilled sufficiently to set the stage for geothermal
development. In various cooperative projects we demonstrated the use of
biotechnology.

Perhaps most dramatically, we put the ocean to work as an alternate
source of energy. Because Hawaii was formed by volcanic eruptions
from the deep-ocean floor, the Islands drop off steeply into the surround-
ing sea. Deep water is much colder than the water of the surface, which
acts as an enormous collector of the sun's rays. Our research focused on
a theory that cold, subsurface ocean water could be pumped up and
made to collide with sun-heated surface water in a controlled chamber,
with usable energy resulting from the heat exchange. This is called

Ocean Thermal Energy Conversion, or OTEC. We demonstrated that OTEC could function not only in a laboratory but in the natural environment of the ocean. For me it was a moving experience to know that we had, for the first time, successfully generated electricity from OTEC in the ocean. I immediately wrote a note to President Carter saying, "What happened today was like the Wright Brothers flying the first aircraft. It didn't fly very far, and it will require improvements in technology, but we proved that it can be done."

Along the way, we brought millions of dollars of research money into Hawaii, creating high-quality work. As part of our effort, we established the Natural Energy Laboratory of Hawaii on the dry, sun-drenched Kona Coast of the Big Island. Its most important feature is a large pipe that follows a particularly steep drop from the coast to the ocean depths.

As a result of our work in alternate energy, we were in the vanguard of the most difficult resource transition facing the global community. This work still goes on in Hawaii today, but to my dismay it was drastically cut back when Ronald Reagan became president. He appointed a director of the U.S. Department of Energy whose goal was to shut the department down. The attitude underlying such political behavior was, to me, exactly the type of short-term thinking that can lead us to disaster.

IN THE PROCESS OF WORKING ON OTEC, we saw that a large amount of energy generated by OTEC is used to pump the cold ocean water to the surface, so we searched for ways to charge this cost to other benefits. I asked the brilliant engineer, Dr. John Craven, how much of a research and development budget he would need to find related uses of cold water. He said $150,000, and I gave him $160,000. Certain species—such as lobster, oysters, and abalone—respond best to a combination of warm sun and cool water, and they rose quickly on our scale of feasibility.

Researchers of abalone asked the State for use of land at the Natural Energy Laboratory. In response, I decided to make land and water systematically available to pioneers in the field of cold-water businesses. The result was the Hawaii Ocean Science and Technology center, next to the Energy Laboratory. These two institutions share the same deep-ocean water source. The water pipe connects to a shared site where the island falls off quickly and steeply into the deep ocean, which means that a minimum of energy and money is spent on pumping the cold water up into the near-shore environment.

We nurtured a range of activities that integrated land and sea. The abalone grew twice as fast as any other abalone in the world. I marveled at such things. Their growth was enhanced by feeding them a fast-growing kelp. At my last National Governors' Association meeting, I made a presentation that I started by asking, "Can anyone name a plant that grows eighteen inches a day?" No one could. The governors were amazed by the story of the growth of kelp.

Another product in a similar vein is spirulina algae, which now is doing well commercially as a high-quality nutritional supplement. As governor, I got to pour the first glass of spirulina into the waters of Kona.

My conscious focus on preserving open space by making the land productive, coupled with an emphasis on freshwater resources, led my Administration to a special emphasis on the broader subject of aquaculture. Again, the windward side of Oahu played a special role, because land had opened up on the northern point of Windward Oahu as a result of the closing of Kahuku Sugar Co. This freed up a great deal of land *and* fresh water. Furthermore, the site was not that far from the University of Hawaii and only a few miles from the Hawaii Institute of Marine Biology at Coconut Island in Kaneohe Bay.

For a time we made great strides in the culture of freshwater prawns, shrimp, oysters, and abalone. I hoped aquaculture would be a major new industry for Hawaii. During my tenure it grew from being virtually nonexistent to a several-million-dollar-a-year resource. It continued to expand thereafter, but as I write, the early progress in aquaculture has stalled. Its value and feasibility have been demonstrated, and the technologies have been worked out. Its future will be determined by a combination of factors—entrepreneurship, market conditions, and public policy regarding the land and water that are being freed up by the demise of sugar and pineapple.

WHILE I SHARED PATTERNS OF THOUGHT with the environmental movement, I sometimes parted ways with various environmental organizations. I often thought in terms of the long-term *use* of resources, and not in terms of conservation for its own sake. This put me at odds with people who opposed any type of environmental change—people who, from my viewpoint, opposed putting unused resources to work for society.

It was to the dismay of some of the environmental organizations that I supported the development of geothermal energy on the Big Island. We conducted feasibility studies and drilled test wells. I believed no single breakthrough could do as much to relieve us of our oil dependency, yet full-scale geothermal development no doubt will have an environmental cost.

In some of our studies, geothermal energy became linked to a second idea that groups within the environmental movement also staunchly opposed. That was the deep-ocean mining of manganese nodules. The global economy is running low on manganese and other trace minerals that are found in abundance in the deep ocean. When cost and demand become high enough, these resources will be mined despite the great ocean depths at which they occur. I worked to position the Big Island as a center for mining and extracting the precious metals, which would have required a carefully designed processing operation.

Again, these ideas may have been ahead of their time, but they will come around again to visit us. I think the most relevant concern will be the balanced and careful use of resources over the long term, and not the preservation of all aspects of the environment as it happens to exist at a particular moment.

As I have indicated, the Department of Planning and Economic Development was the lead agency for this type of thinking. The existence of these two functions in a single governmental department virtually guaranteed that schemes for economic development would be subjected to searching questions from a planning viewpoint. After my terms in office, these functions were reorganized into a department devoted solely to business advocacy[12] and a completely separate Office of Planning within the Governor's Office. I think the result was a loss of balance between economic development and planning, as well as an excessive politicization of the planning function. I believe our original approach, in place from the time of Statehood, was the right one. Economic development leads to enduring changes, which rightly should be planned carefully. Furthermore, the public's positive feeling about planning is a worthwhile asset in itself. Planning should be rational and therefore relatively apolitical, structured in a professional environment that is at an appropriate distance from the governor and his staff. Planning must not only be at an arm's length from politics, but it must *appear* so.

DURING MY LAST TERM OF OFFICE, articles appeared in national publications lambasting Hawaii as having the most anti-business climate in the country. Our complex system of zoning and permitting came in for special criticism. So did the Hawaii State Plan. So did our health care system (later to be held up as a possible national model). So did our extensive

---

[12]Now called the Department of Business, Economic Development and Tourism. As of this writing, the State Planning Office has been reassigned to this department.

unionization of the work force, safety regulation of the work place, and so on.

Given my interest in business, I was extremely unhappy with these criticisms. Mostly they resulted from applying continental modes of thinking to an island society. They showed a lack of understanding of the type of community we are building in Hawaii.

In some instances, our own standards contrasted to unsound practices in other states. As I've noted earlier, there is no point in starting just any business in Hawaii, because of our distance from product markets, the high cost of living, the cost of long-distance ocean shipping, and so on. I opposed schemes for subsidizing business startups or businesses that relocate to Hawaii. Typically, these are proposals for exempting certain operations from taxation, or from environmental regulation, or from employer obligations to employees. If we play favorites with a new business, what are we saying to an existing business that is struggling for viability? If a business is sound, it will be able to do its part. In a national climate that was increasingly devoted to paying court to business, I stuck with our original idea that equal opportunity counted most. The most important issue, again, is fairness.

Business is tough and resilient. I particularly admire the toughness of small business, which tends to create the most new jobs and new activities. Small business is quick to respond to new conditions and new opportunities. It can pull in its belt in lean times. If business has a stable governmental environment, it can creatively adapt to market and economic changes. Accordingly, I sought to provide a stable governmental environment above all.

In the early days of the Democratic Party we were close to small business because of our commitment to an open economy and a level playing field. The criticism often has been made that in Democratic times we went from being heavily dependent on plantation agriculture to being heavily dependent on a tourism industry that has a lot in common with the economics and organization of plantations. I can see why the large destination resorts may strike the eye as a modern variation of the plantation world, but in truth the tourism industry is much more diverse. It lends itself to a continuum of activities, ranging from a package tour to a gathering of philosophers from East and West. The services required for travel and business activities are diverse, and in the information age they become more so—information, in fact, becomes an industry in itself.

In our present uneasy relationship with tourism, we would do well to get a better overview of national and international economics. At one time we were a great manufacturing nation, but much of the industrial production capacity of America has been "hollowed out" by the movement of industry to low-cost overseas labor sources. We have seen this in Hawaii as the industrial-era agriculture of the large plantations has declined. Sugar is phasing out, and pineapple is all but gone. Hawaii had the largest pineapple canneries in the world, and today they are historical curiosities, as our companies went overseas to grow pineapple and process it with low-cost labor.

In the future there will be more and more production of goods outside the United States. We think we have so many imported goods now, but this will accelerate. In response we must become more export-minded. Middle-sized and small businesses in Hawaii can get involved in identifying and supplying export markets. Government has a role to play in assisting with marketing. Just as car manufacturers need to make cars with right-hand drives for the foreign markets, we need to adapt to the overseas customers—giving them the right products in packages of the right color, shape, and size.

The trade deficit is a focus of reports by the U.S. Commerce Department to the National Governors Association. When I asked about the role of tourism in offsetting the much-publicized trade deficit, their answers were skimpy. I said shame on them for not really understanding the importance of tourism, and I would go on to tell my colleagues that visitors from Japan were spending about three times what the average tourist spent, that this spending represented an effective export of services, and that perhaps we in Hawaii were one of the few states that did not have a trade deficit with Japan. While I am concerned about exporting products, much more emphasis now needs to be placed on exporting services, since sixty percent of the American economy now is comprised of services. Tourism is the single biggest of the service industries, not only in Hawaii but throughout the United States. In 1986, when I was still governor, tourism was first, second, or third in the economic base of forty of the fifty states. Tourism was the largest private employer not only in Hawaii but in fourteen states. It was the second largest employer in seventeen other states. In other words, tourism was the number one or number two private employer in well over half the states of the United States.

Foreign visitors conveniently arrive in our country and deliver their wealth. As this is written, tourism from China and Korea is growing rapidly, and Japanese travel to the United States is projected to double by the year 2000. This continuing growth of Asian travel is in many ways sustaining the economy of Hawaii, and we should recognize that fact and work with it.

Perhaps because travel grew so rapidly in Hawaii, and because it became such a huge factor in our economy, people became preoccupied with the downside effects of tourism. In many people's minds it became a bad thing. Some see it as totally out of control. The fact is that we have shaped it extensively by land use zoning, by the organization of labor, by training and educating workers, by development of sites that interpret our history and culture, and so on. We need to continue this process of shaping tourism.

I also think we need to set limits on tourism based on the overall carrying capacity of the environment of Hawaii. As we do these things we can intelligently come to terms with tourism, rather than aimlessly doing battle with it.

One way of understanding the upside potential of tourism is to see that the service economy has resulted in the creation of many, many small businesses. In 1970, Hawaii had 12,000 businesses. By 1980 Hawaii had 20,000 small businesses. That number today is up to nearly 30,000 small businesses.

I ALSO THINK IT IS IMPORTANT to get a clearer understanding of the limits to the role of government in economic development. In Hawaii we have a tradition of highly centralized government that can be traced to Kamehemeha's wars of conquest and the formation of the Hawaiian Kingdom. The plantation economy was spread out widely over the landscape, but the management of it was centralized in the Big Five firms.[13]

From the vantage of our highly centralized State government, there is a temptation to try to remake the economic landscape. Officeholders are constantly racking their brains for the brilliant ideas that will give us the diversity we would like to have.

However, I want to suggest that diversification is indeed happening, and the best way to help it along is for government to know its place. Jobs that are created by government result only from collecting taxes and spending public funds. No matter what we do in the public sector, we do not create a single self-sustaining job.

Businesses are created when an individual or company is willing to

---

[13]To give an obvious example, both the Kingdom and Territorial governments were involved in the importation of labor.

invest in an opportunity to provide goods or services. A business continues only when revenues exceed costs. Jobs in the private sector generate tax money, rather than spend it. Obviously, the creative side of the community is the private sector, and we should respect that fact.

If Republicans sometimes make too much of this point, we Democrats make too little of it. We need to again get anchored in the real tasks of government, which are in education, maintaining the environment, and providing compassionate help to those who genuinely need it. General research and development, and the pursuit of national and international grants, are legitimate government functions in the stages of economic development that precede private initiative. Government also has an appropriate, on-going role in certain forms of marketing, such as travel marketing and the promotion of agricultural products, but in many areas of economic activity we need to see more clearly the right time to get out of the way. We need to recognize successful entrepreneurship and then become more entrepreneurial.

Looking around the United States and Asia, and seeing how international things are becoming, we must ask how Hawaii will make a transition into this new era. What will move us ahead? While we may be tempted to generate government answers, the hard part will be to recognize that the private sector ultimately will create economic change in Hawaii, and entrepreneurs should be left to do what they do best.

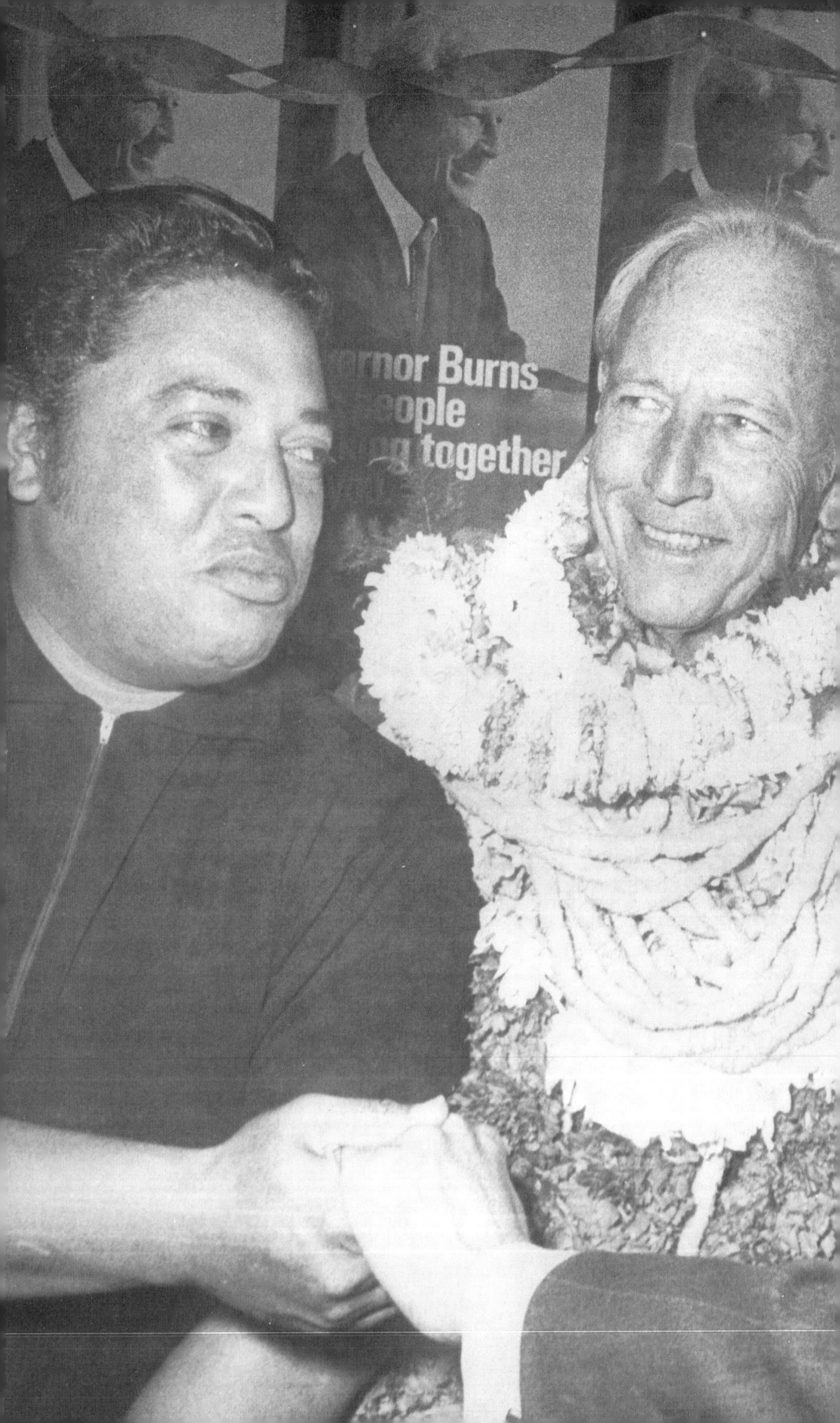
rnor Burns
eople
together

(Preceding pages) Entertainer Zulu greets me, Governor Burns, and my father on a wonderful night in 1970.

(Clockwise, from left) With Susumu Ono during a legislative session. Presenting part of the State Plan. Addressing the Democratic Party.

(Following page, top) I most liked to talk with people in small groups. (Bottom) Jean and I confer with campaign advisers, Gary Caulfield, Dan Ishii, and Walter Dods.

CHAPTER TEN

The People Machine

In 1978, as the first reelection campaign approached, so many people thought I would lose that the expectation of my political demise became conventional wisdom. Supposedly this is a highly uncomfortable position for a politician to be in. Your reputation is at stake. Your friends and supporters are counting on you to win. You must stay in the warmth of the winner's circle. The alternative is to wake up "out in the cold."

The fact was I never felt seriously stressed by trailing in a campaign, nor in the conduct of my office. My answer to stress was to keep politics in perspective. Perspective for me came from paying attention to, and bene-fiting from, the relationships within our family. Each of our three chil-dren was born during legislative sessions, two years apart. In the 1963 Legislature, when I was chairman of the Ways and Means Committee, I became concerned about doing my part to take care of the kids. Instead of socializing around the Capitol, I went home during breaks. I was lucky to live close by, and I would go home even if I could spend only a half hour, and even if we ate hurriedly. Sometimes I would drive up and my kids would be ready with their baseball gloves to throw the ball.

I made it to most of their games and performances. I used to take Wednesday afternoons off from my law practice during the summer to take everyone to the beach, and we would go out on Saturdays and Sundays. When the children were younger, we had impromptu family meetings. Anyone had a right to call a family meeting, and we were all obligated to get together no later than a day after the request was made. Meetings were often about somebody feeling that something unfair had been done to them by someone else in the family. We would talk about what happened, why it happened, and how we could smooth out the aggrieved member's feelings. We told our children that as parents we were not perfect, that parents make mistakes too, but as long as there was love, we would always work things out.

After I became governor, I again became concerned about having time with my children. When we moved from our home in Nuuanu to Washington Place, the children were thirteen, fifteen, and seventeen, respectively. I told my secretary that whenever one of them called, or whenever one came to the Capitol, I was to be notified no matter what I was doing. I wanted my children to always have access to me. I would bring them in between appointments and ask how they were and what was going on. They usually said they just stopped by, but I think they wanted to see me. I think they wanted to be sure that if they needed me, I was going to be available.

My job posed difficulties for them. When I got negative publicity, or when somebody said something about me in their presence, it hit them personally. If their peers said derogatory things, it affected them even more. One of my boys was told by a classmate, "I hope your father gets assassinated." I know they got into fights occasionally over such remarks, and this was one such time.

While the impact on our family was real, it was minimized by our practices. As a general rule, I didn't feel that public life was in conflict with family life, because I had no qualms about giving priority to the family when I was needed. If you are in politics but *don't* take care of your own family, then whatever you have to say about the rest of the community is empty talk.

Everything starts with the family, with those closest to you. You cannot ignore them to look at the bigger picture.

When things at work were not going as well as they might, I relied on an inner sense of calm and order. Typically people worry too much, often about things that work out satisfactorily later on. Worry causes stress, but with all the problems I had I never felt really stressed. You can fool others by presenting a facade of well-being, but you can't fool yourself. There is no substitute for peace of mind. I worked hard and felt I was doing the best I could. When I made mistakes, my anxiety was minimized by knowing I was doing all I was capable of doing.

There are occasional moments when such a job makes you feel burdened, and there are moments when you may sag. But most of the time I felt really good. I was always interested in the challenges I faced. Thanks perhaps to the perpetual optimism that was handed down by my mother, I looked at problems as opportunities to make things better. If problems do not occur, things are left as they are. But if a problem comes up, it is an opportunity to make improvements. You can improve not only on the immediate problem area but on areas around it.

Seeing my work this way, I had no inclination to let down. I found I was blessed with an abundance of energy and stamina. Anyone who wants to be a chief executive should know that the sheer volume of the work requires long hours, no matter how good you are at delegating. I would put in a full day. Then we often had social engagements in the early evening. Almost invariably I would return to the job, either at my State Capitol office or my desk at Washington Place. I would work far into the night and more than occasionally into the early morning hours. When I went to bed, I slept soundly until it was time to get up.

Regardless of how late I worked, whether it was midnight or two-thirty in the morning, I would be up by six thirty or seven at the latest. Ruby Kimoto, my personal secretary, proved invaluable in keeping me productive and on track through the course of this day-night regime. She was in the Capitol office by six in the morning. She knew where I should go, and what I should work on, virtually all the time. She knew how often I should go out into the community, whether I had gone to a particular function in the past, and how much time should be set aside for activities of all types. If I needed to talk with her early in the morning to get organized for a day's work, I knew she was there. She reviewed everything that went out of my office, and she was usually the last person to leave at night.

I kept physically fit as I went. The plumbing is old at Washington Place, and from the time I turned the tap water on until it actually warmed up, I did thirty push-ups. After shaving I did twenty more. I did a hundred to two hundred sit-ups every night. When I walked someplace, I walked quickly. My companions teased me about my pace, but it saved time and helped keep my energy level high.

I HAD WON THE DEMOCRATIC NOMINATION in 1974 with a plurality, meaning I had the largest number of votes but not a majority.[14] Frank Fasi and Tom Gill together had gotten sixty-two percent of the vote. In 1978, Fasi continued to be mayor, which gave him a strong political base, while Tom Gill had retired to law practice. This created a head to head race between me and Frank Fasi. He started with a lead, and Frank was at his political best when running *against* someone.

Two years before my first campaign in 1954, Frank had made his first race. His goal at that time was to knock off the incumbent mayor, Johnny Wilson, who was the grand old man of the Democratic Party. By that time Johnny Wilson was not well, but everyone who knew him was pulling for him. No one wanted to be seen with Frank, but Frank

---

[14] In round numbers, I had gotten 36 percent of the 1974 primary vote, Fasi 32 percent, and Gill 30 percent. David McClung and a fifth candidate, Henry deFries, got the balance.

nonetheless beat Wilson and won the primary, only to lose in the general to Republican Neal S. Blaisdell. After that Fasi served briefly in the Territorial Senate and for four years on the City Council, but he spent most of his energy for sixteen years getting elected mayor, which he finally did in 1968.

Fasi campaigned constantly, and he had a sizable following. He used his power of incumbency at City Hall to raise money and marshal his political appointees to work on his campaign. Nonetheless he positioned himself as the candidate of change and me as the candidate of "the machine." In Frank's delivery, these two words were spelled with capital letters—The Machine.

The words, The Machine, suggest a chief engineer who is in charge of an unthinking, mechanical apparatus. Presumably everyone is either a "cog in the machine" or being ground up by it. Frank did not invent the phrase, but he certainly popularized it in Hawaii. In the story of The Machine, as it was developed, there was a single "well-oiled" force that had propelled first Governor Burns and then me forward. This impression of a monolithic force typically was not subjected to checks on reality, such as the fact that David McClung also had run in the 1974 Democratic Primary, or—a second example—that I was actively dedicated to opening up the ranks of the Democratic Party. The diverse nature of the Democratic Party never really came across, and Fasi sold the public to a certain extent on the label.

My own perception of the Democratic Party organization was much different, but I readily will grant that the grassroots party organization played a major role in winning elections.

The most organizationally challenging events came late in the campaign. Bob Oshiro came up with the idea of a rally on an unprecedented scale. He set it for Aloha Stadium, which has 50,000 seats. His bold choice of locations meant we risked falling on our faces, because the stadium is stark when the seats are empty. The night before the rally, I went out to the stadium after my usual campaign activities were over. I remember it was quite late, and I couldn't believe what I saw. Campaign workers were going at it by the thousands—a total of seven thousand workers, I was later told. They had hundreds of barbecue fires going, cooking the chicken and meat for the *bento* boxes. In all they made 60,000 *bento* boxes. The cooking and packing was a tremendous process in itself. I talked to a chef who was used to preparing fifteen hundred meals for a banquet, and he was staggered that we had prepared forty times that number.

Thank goodness Aloha Stadium was filled the next evening, and we needed all those *bento* boxes. The people who worked, and those who came, gave me a tremendously warm feeling. It was the largest political gathering in the history of Hawaii. The comedian Frank DeLima performed, and later he told me the rally was the first time he had ever played before such a large group, and that was the night his career in show business really took off. Don Ho, Zulu, and dozens of others donated their performances as well.

Two Sundays before the primary, a poll came out in *The Honolulu Advertiser,* which showed me still running ten points behind Frank Fasi. We had a meeting that morning, and Dr. Dan Tuttle, the political science professor, came to help us evaluate the poll. I'm still unsure how accurate the poll was, but overall at that moment things looked really bad.

If the poll was accurate, it was a blessing in disguise, because the publicity of the poll motivated people to work even harder than they had. Bob Oshiro's response was to give our grassroots workers another challenge. He set a telephone calling system in motion in the last week. Some people called their families. Some called friends and acquaintances as well. Bob got reports and kept running tallies of the calls that were being made. I was told this effort reached a hundred thousand people in just a few days. Of course some people got three or four calls, but this was not science. This was enthusiasm. The energy and feeling were what mattered.

Our "machine" was made up of the many grassroots Democrats who came out for the stadium rally and participated in the last-minute drive to victory. Typically a supporter felt strongly about the leadership I was providing or, more broadly, the leadership the Democratic Party had provided over the years. This person might have started in the coffee hours of 1964, or 1970 or 1974, but it was someone who really understood the idea of building the future. It was a person who would make sacrifices if they knew their children's future would be made better. Our machine was the grassroots worker and the Democratic Party member. It was made up of ordinary people in the community—all kinds of people who did all kinds of work. On election day I won the Democratic nomination for the second time.

THE HEAD-TO-HEAD CONTEST with Frank F. Fasi was a turning point in my twelve years as elected governor, because it resulted in my having a more secure political position than I had previously enjoyed. I think Frank said a lot of things and did a lot of things because he wanted so badly to become governor, and I stood in his way.[15] Years later when I left office I played in a golf tournament with him. I came in late that night to the tournament dinner, and he was already seated. When I sat down I saw him get up as if he were leaving. I thought, "I've done something to offend him," but he came back with sushi and food for me. It was a warm gesture on his part, which I appreciated very much. From then on, his treatment of me was different, and I have enjoyed a courteous relationship with him.

After turning back Fasi in the primary, the general election of 1978 was the easy part, just as it had been in 1970 and 1974. My Republican opponent was a young State senator, John Leopold, who relocated to the Mainland after losing by a wide margin.[16]

I was fortunate in political terms, and so was the Democratic Party. I closed out my career in elective politics by winning my third and final four-year term as governor in 1982. In the primary, I survived a challenge from Lieutenant Governor Jean Sadako King. In the general, Frank Fasi ran as an independent, and D.G. "Andy" Anderson ran for the Republicans. My forty-five percent of the vote was described as a landslide by the press. Where I might have been in a position of overstaying my welcome, the victory in the final gubernatorial campaign of 1982 occurred with relative ease.

Starting with 1954, in the course of my essentially unplanned political career, I was on the ballot in twenty-four elections, including primaries and generals, plus a twenty-fifth election as delegate to the Constitutional Convention of 1968. Some of the election campaigns stand out vividly in my memory, while others do not. I was fortunate to win all twenty-five of them in the course of serving continuously for thirty-two years.[17]

---

[15] He subsequently ran for governor as an independent in 1982 and 1994, to no avail.

[16] The Republican candidate in 1966 and 1974, Randolph Crossley, likewise moved to the Mainland.

[17] Territorial House - 1954, 1956; Territorial Senate - 1958; Special Statehood Election, Senate - 1959; State Senate - 1962, 1964, 1966, 1968; Constitutional Convention - 1968; Lieutenant Governor - 1970; Governor - 1974, 1978, 1982.

CHAPTER ELEVEN

Managing Money

LIBERALISM THRIVED FOR A LONG TIME in American politics as a result of the strength and vibrancy of the economy. Economic growth yielded ever-expanding tax revenues, which provided government with the money for social programs. In this process, liberalism developed an unfortunate identification with a big-spending approach to government. Today the size and role of government are being critically re-examined, typically from a politically conservative viewpoint. But from personal experience I can say the politics of frugality need not be based on arch-conservatism. The supposed father figure of present-day conservatism, former President Reagan, overspent on the arms race. While doing this he actually cut taxes and caused a dangerous increase in the budget deficit.

I was governor of Hawaii in the lean years that led up to President Reagan's tenure in office, as well as the first six years of his eight-year term.[18] During much of this period, the performance of Hawaii's economy was flat, and so were tax revenues. It was a good thing for me politically, and for my inherent peace of mind, that I had a deeply ingrained commitment to be careful about spending. Insofar as I can be categorized by political labels, I would say I am a social liberal and a fiscal conservative. The core of my attitudes about money came from my upbringing. It may sound simplistic, but there is an accurate analogy between a family budget and a government budget. In both instances, you have only so much to spend. You can't spend more than you have for long, or you wind up in trouble. My family watched our resources with care. We made hard decisions about what mattered most.

Because my father had inculcated me with a concern for the interests of the coming generation, as governor I felt deeply obligated to not adversely affect the financial future of Hawaii. Being fiscally sound meant not saddling the next generation with debt.

---

[18]I served from 1973 to 1974 as acting governor, then from 1974 to 1986 as governor, substantially overlapping Reagan's two terms, which ran from 1980 to 1988.

It was the need to keep the budget in balance that led me to often say "no" to new government spending programs. I actively supported programs for the truly needy that provided a social safety net, because I believed we have an obligation to provide adequately and humanely for poor, disabled, and handicapped people. But I was wary of ideas that had the potential of reducing self-sufficient people—or potentially self-sufficient people—to a state of dependency on government. Society doesn't help people by doing everything for them. I go back to our relationships within our families. We love our children, but we don't do everything for them. We can't *afford* to do everything for them, but in any case we want them to grow up to be independent.

Government is at its best when it gives people tools and encouragement, when government says, "You can do it, and you're going to be stronger as a result." Yet as governor I experienced continuous pressure to subsidize, or take over, the community work traditionally performed by volunteer-based organizations, always with the goal of making their services bigger and better. Such organizations stretch small amounts of community funding to cover a wide range of needs. These volunteer efforts bring passionate concerns to bear that government, by its nature, cannot sustain. Also, volunteer groups often have value orientations that are not appropriate to government in a pluralistic society.

In their zeal, volunteer groups present compelling, sometimes heart-wrenching rationales for public funding, but when volunteer groups get out of their inventive, impassioned mode and into the realm of governmental budgeting they tend to lose their way. Therefore when I looked at community-based volunteer work I would return to my basic concept. By trying to do too much, government can end up crippling people. It is possible to give volunteer groups too much government support, and to end up consuming them.

Government must focus on doing its existing tasks well. When I rescinded Governor Burns' freeze on hiring people into new jobs, I took my first significant step toward sharing responsibility for the performance of State government in order to get the most return on taxpayers' resources. When I went out to visit State workers, I talked with them about how important they are. As an alternative to being silent or merely grumbling, I urged people to speak up. "No matter what you are doing," I said, "you know your jobs better than anyone else." I urged them to give their best effort in their capacity as experts in their areas of work. I told them to be candid with me and with their supervisors, and to say why some ideas made sense while others didn't. I stressed to them, "Speak up in terms of providing better service to the public, and not in terms of your own convenience."

I told them that after such discussion, everyone had to function as a team. "Pull together. Work together." We hired relatively few new people. We usually promoted from within. We also reassigned people from within. I found highly capable people were stagnating in top-level jobs. They would master their tasks, come to know their jobs too well, do the same things over and over, and then lose their creativity. Civil servants can't be laid off, but they can be rejuvenated. I found that a reassignment to a new position could have the effect of a new job. It gave people new challenges, new perspectives, and new energy.

You recall that collective bargaining in the public sector was just starting in my early years as governor. In our negotiations for pay, I constantly stressed fair play and equal treatment. What I did for one person, I tried to do for everyone. Unions fear that if they settle for a certain amount, another union may get a better package by holding out longer. I told my negotiators to tell every collective bargaining unit, and every government union member, that everyone would be treated fairly and equally. Worker expectations inevitably exceeded our resources, but I refused to agree to settlements that would push the State onto shaky financial ground. Most of the public unions endorsed me over and over, but during my tenure I took a teachers' strike, a university strike, a blue-collar worker strike, and a brief walkout of white-collar workers. Certainly not everyone got what they wanted, but neither did anyone lose their jobs.

In 1979, through the collective bargaining process, we went through a rugged negotiation with the Firemen's Union. Eventually we reached a settlement that seemed eminently fair. From the guidelines that resulted, we settled with twelve of the thirteen bargaining units. The thirteenth, made up mostly of janitorial workers from the United Public Workers Union, went on strike. As I analyzed their strike demands, I saw they were trying to jump the parameters set by the other contracts. I dug in my heels. The strike dragged on. The schools were closed. Hospitals, airports, and other institutions were piled high with trash. On the seventeenth day of the strike, with my patience at an end, I held a press conference. I bluntly described my view of the strike. I mobilized parents, students, and educators to clean up the schools and resume class. I stood by my principle of dealing with all the bargaining units in the same general way. An agreement was reached, and the strike ended.

It was one of many instances where I tried to offset the chaotic nature of the times by stressing equal treatment for all. Personnel policies don't sound exciting, but they're important. When you ask people to work harder and give more, you have to convince them that everyone is in the same boat. I insisted on as many jobs as possible being quality, full-time jobs with complete benefit packages, including Hawaii's pioneering health care insurance. I avoided the creation of part-time jobs, temporary jobs, and contract jobs, all of which tend to create sub-categories of people with differing interests. Such sub-categories erode the structure of the government workforce and distort the readily apparent rationale for positions and pay. Unusual categories of work have an extra potential for favoritism, or even the possible appearance of favoritism. Resentment is the result.[19]

I forfeited my own salary increases. Compensation studies told me that department directors and deputies needed raises if government was to maintain a semblance of competitiveness with the private sector. Since the governor's pay is at the top of the scale, pay raises for department directors would push the salary of the governor up. This perplexed me. I was a temporary occupant of the office, with an obligation to maintain an appropriate pay structure for future governors. But I also believed that when I ran for the office I had made a personal commitment to serve at the salary that was in effect when I was elected. When I ran for the job, I knew what it paid. I felt I had made a compact with the voting public to serve at that salary level for the term to which I was elected.

I resolved the issue by supporting an increase for department directors and deputies, as well as for the office of governor, but I satisfied my conscience by contributing my increase in salary to charity. At the time I kept this quiet. I didn't want it to be exploited politically, so I said nothing. Even when political opponents were attacking me and criticizing me for supposedly taking a pay raise, I kept my course of action to myself. Although I gained no immediate political advantage from my solution, it helped me nonetheless. To do a job, you can't have a serious conflict within yourself. You have to deal with your conscience first, and you have to feel good about what you do. If I was asking other people to sacrifice, I had to start with myself.

Every time there was a pay increase I diverted the margin of the increase to charity until the next election, which in my view created a new compact between me and the voters. I froze my retirement benefits

---

[19]The exception to this rule was the creation of summer jobs for students, which I felt were both educational and socially desirable.

at the salary level of my first year as elected governor; I received no increase in retirement benefits for the twelve years that were to follow. Friends told me I had a responsibility to my family to take all the retirement benefits I could legally get, that my retirement did not belong to me alone, but to my family.

I had myself insured so my family's future would be secure if something happened to me while I was governor. By 1970, when I had closed my law practice to serve full time in public office, I had reached a point where I could be selective about my clients and about what I did. I possibly gave up my top earning years to be in office, but I was confident that when I was finished with public life I could pick up the pieces of my law practice and still perform demanding work and provide for my family. That has been the case.

In the public sphere, the ultimate object of our fiscal strategizing was a steady flow of cash to create stability in government. Even if revenues are unstable, we must have stable governmental operations. Before I became governor, I had seen tax revenues fluctuate widely. Some years revenues grew as much as twenty percent, but in other years revenues hardly grew. *I learned you can only really manage in good times.*

This principle is the key to controlling the government budget. In good times you can set priorities and also put money aside. While some programs undeniably need more money over time, and new initiatives must be made to respond to new situations, the long-term implications of increased spending on government operations must be weighed with great care. When you fund an operating program one year, it is difficult to cut that program the next year. You have elevated people's expectations for service, and new government personnel now depend on the program for their livelihood. Therefore, in a good year, if more money was to be spent, I preferred one-time or short-term commitments, such as repair and maintenance projects, research and development projects, or acquisition of land to be held for the long term. By not locking into recurring commitments in the euphoria of good times, you are in a much better position to cope with the inevitable downturn.

In bad times you have to survive. At best, you will survive in a humane and intelligent way with an absolute minimum of hurt or injustice done to others. Hopefully, you will survive, as I did, without laying people off their jobs.

If the chief executive strikes the wrong balance, and increases spending too much as the result of a good year (or good years), everyone has to cut back when money gets tight. At the National Governors' Association meetings, other governors would talk about having to make big cutbacks in programs and massive layoffs of personnel. They asked me why Hawaii was immune. I told them I had taken care of the problem two to three years earlier, when times were good. Again, there is a simple but profound analogy between government spending and the expenditures we make in our personal lives. If you have years of good income, you should set some aside for the years when you will not be able to work. Maybe your employer will go bankrupt, you will be unemployed, or your job will change. Someday you will have to retire.

The concept of managing in good times is the opposite of what government officials are tempted to do, and what almost invariably occurs. When revenues increase, legislators say, "We're having a good year. Now we can spend." They have ideas about what government can do, and they want credit with the voters for doing something.

My experience as Senate Ways and Means chairman had taught me it's difficult for the Legislature to hold the line on spending. I always remembered when my fellow Democrats walked out on me when I refused to budget money that wasn't there. Even when legislators make a commitment to fiscal responsibility, it's difficult for legislators to accurately assign program costs. If the plan is to spend a hundred dollars, do you in reality need to spend every one of those hundred dollars? Or should you spend only ninety-five? Could you make do with less? The real savings have to come from the execution of the budget, by carefully balancing real costs with what you know to be the intended, uninterrupted service of the program.

In 1977, during my first term, some members of the Legislature made motions to constrain a governor's constitutional right to hold back on spending money that had been authorized by the Legislature. My budget director, Eileen Anderson,[20] went before the Legislature and said in effect, "The governor says to be our guest, but you should first understand what has happened. In less than three years' time, he has saved about *three hundred and forty million dollars* off what you authorized. If he hadn't done that we would have come up extremely short of funds. If you are going to pass your amendment, you will have to take the direct responsibility for being solvent that goes with it, and you will have to make the hard decisions." The legislators quickly backed off.

Lately, in response to the fiscal crisis of the 1990s, there is talk of creating a "rainy day fund." The most painfully obvious point is the impos-

---

[20] Soon to be elected mayor of Honolulu for one term, defeating incumbent Frank F. Fasi.

sibility of creating such a fund when you're out of money. The idea also is flawed by the inherent supposition that such a fund would tide government through a rainy day. How long is a rainy day? Hawaii's economy declined in the recession of the early 1990s and has never gotten back into a real growth mode. Therefore what we need is a level of spending that is workable over long periods, regardless of economic fluctuation. As nearly as possible, recurring expenditures should match recurring revenues. Non-recurring revenues should be saved or dedicated to non-recurring expenditures. The idea of a "rainy day" fund could merely create an illusion of security when our level of spending is actually too high. When such a fund ran out, we would again be in deep trouble.

We must guard against diminishing the future of society by yielding to short-term fiscal solutions in an atmosphere of crisis. One short-term temptation is spending special funds to deal with general-fund costs, which amounts to an erosion of society's dedicated savings. A second temptation is selling off basic resources, such as land. Selling land that can be used for parks, open space, or agriculture amounts to selling resources that we should hold for future generations. It is land that we should not think of as belonging to ourselves in the present. Rather, we hold it as stewards.

There is an increasingly apparent relationship between government stability based on skillful fiscal management and the healthy functioning of the economy. The preponderance of economic analysis is national in scope, but there are wide fluctuations in the performance of smaller economies by region. In this regard Hawaii is a region unto itself. On a State level, keeping public construction moving, and keeping government employment stable, are vitally important to maintaining consumer confidence and also maintaining the willingness of the private sector to invest capital.

Government stability is important to the orderly development of the private sector in even broader, more long-range terms. Because business is the creative economic force in our society, and because business needs to know the rules it is working under, it needs to know that government costs will be relatively stable. Business is hurt by wildly fluctuating government costs. The business environment is hurt when taxes go up, especially on short notice. By the same token, I believe business does not particularly benefit from taxes going down, nor does it need special tax incentives.

Young office-seekers may react by thinking, "This business of fiscal responsibility may be the right thing, but will it get me elected?" I survived the many times I said "no" to spending. In a modest way I capitalized on the issue of living within our means. I asked voters to reflect on why we should not spend more than we had, and that if they agreed with my policies they should return me to office. The voting public seemed to like what I was doing and supported it.

After my successor John D. Waihee went to his first national governors' conference, he called me and said, "I want to thank you for leaving me a surplus of money. My colleagues all tell me their predecessors spent the money and left them with nothing." I appreciated that call. In Hawaii today, voters stop me on the street and say, "I used to get angry with you for not spending money, but now I understand what you were doing." They particularly volunteer favorable comments when news comes out about financial problems.

My savings of $340 million in less than three years averaged out to well over a hundred million dollars a year on a budget that then was in the billion-dollar range. This amounted to a savings of over ten percent of the budget. My experience therefore tells me that we can weather the hard times of the present day. To despair is to further discourage economic activity, which has its own adverse effect on tax revenues. We need the genuine optimism that comes from understanding history, which says we can successfully pull together and persevere.

IF WE DEFINE STEWARDSHIP as the proper management of resources, we are not only more likely to manage government funds properly, but also make the right decisions as regulators of the private financial world. Nationally, the 1980s and early 1990s were a time not only of soaring government debt but also of corporate and consumer debt. American society lived off the future by burdening the next generation.

One of the most chilling developments of this period was the national collapse of enormous sectors of the savings and loan industry. It resulted in a Federal bailout costing over a hundred billion dollars.

As elsewhere, Hawaii had evolved a two-tiered system of thrift institutions. One tier was regulated by, and also insured by, the Federal Deposit Insurance Corporation.[21] The second tier, known as industrial loan companies, was not insured by FSLIC, nor was it regulated to FSLIC standards. While the industrial loan companies paid better returns, they were conceived of as a higher risk, although it's doubtful that many of the depositors understood this.

---

[21]The FSLIC since has consolidated into the Federal Deposit Insurance Corporation, often referrred to by the initials FDIC.

Early in my first term, one of Hawaii's twenty or so industrial loan companies failed in Hawaii. I shut it down as it was headed toward insolvency. In the aftermath I worked with the Legislature, the industry, and State and Federal regulators to set up an entity that we called the Thrift Guaranty Corporation, with the goal of creating a greater measure of security for depositors. We did not know it then, but our problems were far from over. The State's regulatory agency (newly named the Department of Commerce and Consumer Affairs), by then all too acutely aware of the possibility of insolvency, found ongoing problems in several more of the industrial loan companies. We worked with these companies to cure their problems and put them on a sound financial basis.

I knew principals of these companies well. Some were personal friends, and the telephone calls were flying. I naturally wanted to believe the best of the businesses of people I knew well, but I had an obligation as governor to listen to my regulators with a clear and objective mind. I would particularly credit the strong, even-handed role played by Mary Bitterman, then director of Commerce and Consumer Affairs; and Donna Tanoue, then a special deputy attorney general assigned to Ms. Bitterman, and subsequently commissioner of Financial Institutions.

In an agonizing decision, we decided to close two small industrial companies. We used assets of the Thrift Guaranty Corporation to make the depositors whole, but this again was not the entire story. Mary Bitterman found two more companies were not in compliance, and these were much larger than the first two. Finally, reluctantly, we deemed their steps toward compliance to be inadequate. We put both of these larger companies into receivership. This was even more difficult than our previous decision because by this time the Thrift Guaranty fund was insufficient to cover the depositors. The best we could do in the short term was to see that depositors got a third of their money back. We opted against holding a "fire sale" to liquidate the assets of the companies. Instead we proceeded with a sort of deliberate haste to liquidate the assets in such a way as to come closer to realizing their real value. Following this course, and with the help of good court-appointed receivers, we covered the remaining two-thirds of the deposits over the next year to eighteen months.

One day a rumor began to spread that Honolulu Federal, or HonFed,[22] was also going under. The rumor spread crazily. Depositors materialized everywhere, lining up in a classic panic to withdraw their savings. The fact that HonFed was insured and regulated by the Federal Savings and

---

[22] Since acquired by Bank of America

Loan Insurance Corporation made no difference, nor did the fact that HonFed was financially sound. We did what we could, but nothing mattered more than the fact that HonFed kept its doors open and paid out enormous sums to its depositors, dollar for dollar. People—oftentimes frail, elderly people—carried off tens of thousands of dollars in grocery bags, sometimes under the protective eye of the police. Airplane after airplane brought huge sums of cash in to cover the run. In all, HonFed paid out well over $40 million before people realized the institution was sound. Finally the panic subsided.

While all these events were occurring we discovered new Federal legislation that had the potential for achieving what we had hoped to achieve with the Thrift Guaranty Corporation. The new Federal law, passed by Congress in 1980, allowed industrial loan companies to come under the FSLIC, provided they met its regulatory standards. Mary Bitterman and Donna Tanoue and their staffs worked furiously with the FSLIC regional office and the remaining sixteen companies to bring everyone up to standard.

We passed a bill through the 1983 Legislature setting this new, high standard for all thrift institutions in Hawaii, and all sixteen remaining companies qualified for FDIC guarantees with the active guidance of our team. From that moment on, all thrift institutions were regulated to the highest available standards and all deposits were insured by the Federal government. We were the first of the fifty states to take advantage of the new Federal law, and if this had been widely used around the country, perhaps the country would not have experienced the financial disaster that ensued.

In the moment of truth, not one of Hawaii's savings and loans failed its responsibility to depositors. I am deeply pleased by this fact, but to this day I feel badly for those people whose institutions were closed—persons who believed they were performing reasonably well but who were hurt by my decisions. I hope they have come to appreciate that I had an obligation to the general community that was inherent in the administration of fair and impartial government.

FROM TIME TO TIME, SCHEMES TO LEGALIZE GAMBLING have come up in Hawaii, as they have around the country. In Hawaii, they always have been shelved. Large groups within the community have opposed legalized gambling on principle. As I write, the State government is short of revenues, and talk of gambling now is much in the air. In my view, this is a time when we need to stick to principle. I am opposed to any type of legalized gambling.

Gambling schemes bring us face to face with the issue of what kind of community we want to leave to our children and grandchildren. We want our young people to learn that achievement comes from hard work and patience, but gambling teaches them to look for the stroke of luck. We want people to be frugal and take care of their families, but gambling poses a constant temptation to waste money and ignore real-world needs. When people lose "just a little," they go back to recoup. Then they lose more. People who can least afford it are the most vulnerable.

While gambling may look like an easy way to solve our fiscal problems, it won't work that way. In fact gambling is potentially injurious to the existing tax base. Travel to Hawaii always has been a wholesome experience. Visitors readily bring their families. While it may be true that organized gambling can be regulated to some extent, I do not believe we can have it and still keep out the big-time criminal elements. If that happens, the quality of life in Hawaii will be degraded, and Hawaii's attractiveness to the visitors we want will be diminished.

Casino gambling and shipboard gambling would result in dislocating visitor expenditures. The money now spent on tours, entertainment, shops, and restaurants would be spent on casinos. Entertainment would be particularly hard hit, because gambling not only takes money but time—time that people now use to listen to music, watch performances, go to movies, and experience the culture and history of Hawaii.

Similarly, gambling in the form of a lottery is unlikely to be a new revenue windfall. If it is true that a lottery might yield an increase in tax dollars during the initial excitement, it is also true that people are not stupid. If the lottery did not pay its players well and often, it would mean the State was pocketing the money. Players would pull back, and the bubble would deflate. Conversely, if the lottery paid its players a lion's share of the "pot," little revenue would be left.

We can manage our fiscal problems by being careful, sharing the short-term pain, and keeping an eye on our long-term goals. We can make it through. In the meantime, we should remember that when an issue of principle is the least convenient it may be the most important.

I GENERALLY HAD GOOD RELATIONS with the Legislature. I understood the legislative process and respected it. I also worked hard at my relationships. When I sent proposals down to the Legislature, I let legislators know, "I want to develop these ideas with you." Oftentimes I would not even make a formal proposal, but I would talk with them and say, "It would be good if we could have such-and-such kind of thing." I wanted them to have a lot of room to shape ideas and also to receive credit. An idea that was mine would become ours, and sometimes it would become theirs alone.

I tried not to raise public expectations until I had a pretty good idea that a range of feasible solutions was available. I avoided telling the Legislature they had to do something that was impossible. In political games of one-upsmanship, this practice has the effect of implying that legislators are bad people for not being able to respond. It sets off the vicious cycle of one branch of government blaming another branch of government. By way of contrast, I constantly tried to reason with legislators. I took the approach that we were all in situations together.

Jack Burns had a good relationship with the Legislature by following the principles I have described. While times became more contentious during my tenure, these principles also served me well. The Legislature's public hearing process is one of the most important features of democratic practice. I had been greatly impressed by its workings as a legislator, and as governor I was aware that I did not have the direct benefit of hearings. The Administration was a vehicle for generating ideas and organizing information, but the impact of ideas can only be gauged through public hearings. An idea that worked well in California might be revealed as premature in Hawaii, or in conflict with our diverse lifestyles.

Politics today seems more and more dominated by special issues and narrow concerns. We saw this vividly in recent legislative sessions when the issue of same-sex marriage dominated the news while serious, far-reaching issues seemed to receive little or no attention. In the background, the Democratic Party organization (and probably the Republican Party as well) tends increasingly to be a conglomeration of single-issue concerns and single-issue activists. In a two-day convention, the Party approves a platform that many Party members expect the Legislature to enact into legislation, the quicker the better. While the interest and zeal of these people may be admirable, I try to tell Party people to realize they have a limited perspective. The Legislature's public hearing process is the best mechanism for getting broad public input and putting the brakes on ideas that are supported by the few.

Again, what we need is to set a broad direction and move toward it. Lately I have become aware that the legislative leadership and the governor meet only rarely. This suggests to me that the dialogue that underlies broad progress on public policy is not occurring. During legislative sessions, which run about four months, I met quietly with legislators anywhere from one to several times a week. I routinely had breakfast meetings with the House and Senate leadership. The legislative leadership brought in members in whatever combination they chose. These members expressed a wide range of concerns, and I listened. As a former legislator, I knew that legislators are in touch with their communities. They have their antennae out. If you respect that fact when you are governor, you can get excellent cues from legislators, anticipate problems, and head them off.

On only a few occasions did I have serious differences with them. One arose over my views on how to carefully manage the State Employee's Retirement System. Specifically the issue was the duration of appointments to the board of directors, which governs the Retirement System. As government grew and time passed, the Retirement System accumulated enormous assets that had to be managed so that, in the future, they would cover comparably large obligations.

I thought the existence of this huge sum of money created temptations for people to finance their favorite investment schemes. It holds a potential for abuse similar to other pension and retirement funds around the country. A retirement system can be scrutinized and regulated, but the clarity of purpose and integrity of the board of directors cannot be legislated. Either you have the right people or you don't.

Seeing the potential for temptation, I tried to head off trouble before it started. I reasoned that directors should serve only one six-year term, even though the law allowed for a person to serve two terms. With overlapping appointments, one long term provided a good mixture of experience and new ideas. I reasoned that the intoxication of dealing with so much money would be most likely to set in if people stayed on for a second term, which would mean serving not six but twelve years. In twelve years board members become fixtures, and they tend to become "experts" who begin to cross the line between policy-making and administration. Such people also can become repositories of glowing stories about the future of this or that speculative investment.

I made a decision that I would not reappoint anyone to the Retirement System board. Nonetheless everyone wanted to be reappointed. I made it clear that my position was not personal, that it was a policy, and that in the future I would have the same policy for everyone. Everyone accepted the policy except for one individual. This person went to his friends in the Senate, who were charged with confirming gubernatorial appointments. Influential senators came to see me and wanted me to reappoint this particular director. I told them no. The greater the pressure they exerted on me, the more I wondered why this person wanted to be reappointed, so I did not budge. Since senators are elected to four-year terms they are not used to the word "no." As a result, there was some anger, but we went on with other business.

IN THE 1982 LEGISLATIVE SESSION, a controversy sprang up over the Federal government's special impact aid to education. Hawaii traditionally had received payments from the Federal government as one of the places that is especially impacted by the presence of military dependents. The Reagan Administration threatened to cut out impact aid, and a group of State senators led by Neil Abercrombie decided the best response was retaliation. They passed a bill that said that if impact aid funds were cut off, the families of military dependents had to pay a special educational fee for their children to attend public school. In the mood of the moment, the bill passed. Perhaps Neil thought that since I had supported residency requirements in welfare, I would go along with this way of treating people who were, for the most part, short-term residents of Hawaii. However, I reminded him and other supporters of the bill that the children in question had not asked to be born into military families. Although we wanted to control in-migration, once people were here, I said, they have to all be treated alike. I said the teachers were obligated to teach equality, to teach that all have a right to equal treatment, and that if the law stood it would be difficult for teachers to stand before their classes and tell children that, regardless of background, they were all being treated as equals. Therefore, I said, I was vetoing their bill.

Neil came to see me with the head of the teachers' union to urge me to sign the bill. I responded by saying that as good liberals they should be ashamed of themselves. I said I had originally run for office to put an end to second-class citizenship, and I was not going to sit back and watch a category of children be victimized by discrimination. These children needed the same access to education as everyone else. It didn't matter that their parents didn't vote. I told the union man that if his members were to teach the doctrine of equality, their union could not differentiate between people. If we started down this path, I said, we would find other reasons to discriminate against other groups, and we would be lost.

MY MOTHER WOULD ALWAYS WATCH for the light to be on in my study, or at the Capitol. If it was on, she knew I was working, and she would stay awake out of lifelong habit. A buzzer connected her room at Washington Place to ours, and one morning the buzzer rang about six-thirty. Jeannie and I found my mother lying on the floor, very pale. She had fallen. She moved only with great difficulty. When I asked her when this happened, she said it was about five-thirty.

I told her, "That was an hour ago. Why didn't you buzz us earlier?"

She said, "You were working until early this morning, and you needed your rest."

When we took her to the hospital, we found she had fractured her pelvis and both legs. Her fall permanently limited her mobility, but she nonetheless remained positive and cheerful. Her hands were always moving, doing things for others. She took great pleasure in making things and giving them away. Whether it was pin cushions or pot holders, artificial flowers or a cover for a tissue box, she made things by the hundreds.

Whenever she met somebody, or somebody came over, she would have a gift for them that she had made herself. She bought yarn in huge boxes. One night, she was trying to transform her huge box of yarn into rolls, and it was getting tangled as it came out. I sat and held the yarn while she rolled it. I listened to her talk, as I had when I was a child. As I listened, I marveled at her persistent good cheer in the face of such discomfort.

The cultural traditions my mother knew best were the traditions of early twentieth-century Japan. She was one of the many first-generation immigrants who came to Hawaii and perpetuated the cultural practices of the old country. As a result, if we went out on New Year's Eve, we would be home before midnight. Bamboo and pine decorated the doorway (as they do still). We ate *soba* noodles and popped firecrackers on the stroke of twelve. Then we would bathe, dress in new clothes, and at two-thirty in the morning we would go to the Koto Hiro Jinsha temple in Palama and say a prayer for the New Year. As time passed, Japan changed, but the immigrant settlers in Hawaii were essentially unaware of it, or not part of it. Occasionally cultural traditions have been carried forward in Hawaii that are no longer practiced in Japan. The sticky rice-based *mochi* is pounded by hand on New Year's Day in Hawaii, but this colorful and laborious process long since has been assigned to machines in Japan. We fly cloth carps on Boy's Day here, although this is no longer done in our country of origin. In all these practices, and many more, my mother was traditionally Japanese. She did not speak much English—she could understand a little, but not very much—and she had difficulty conversing with somebody unless they spoke Japanese.

From the time I was little, I was never scolded for doing anything wrong. Instead she told me what was right. I always knew that when I needed support, she would be there. She never saw bad or evil in people, not only with us children, but with everyone. She always looked for the silver lining, and she moved us to look in that direction as well. She started each new day by praying. "Thank you God for ... " and she would recite the names of each member of the family, and then recite the names of friends. Even in her most senior years, when she was in a wheelchair, she continued to go to the Senior Citizen's Center. She would listen to the complaints of the elderly people and say, "Oh, but you had some good times too. You had pleasant moments, didn't you?"

After we left Washington Place, Jeannie continued to take personal care of my mother, which was not easy, because mother was bedridden. She was diabetic, and her foot had to be amputated. Finally mother needed intensive care to the point where we had to move her to a nursing home, and then to a hospital. The doctor told us she could be kept alive only by putting her on life-support machines, and that she would not be able to converse or even recognize us—she would be inert and unknowing. He asked us to think together and let him know what we wanted him to do. My brother and sisters and I got together. I said *okaasan* had had a good life. She had given us so much, and it would be asking too much of her to just keep her alive in an unfeeling state, just because we couldn't let go. We all decided that if need be we had to let go as an expression of our love and respect for her. I told the doctor to make her comfortable, but not to do anything to try to prolong her life. Within fifteen minutes she was gone. It was as though she wanted us to tell her it was all right.

When my mother passed away, the kids got together and we talked. I told them that when I was little, I thought mother was funny, because the things that I enjoyed eating, the delicious, tasty, *ono* things, mother didn't care for. She would say, "You folks go ahead and eat." I said she saw light even in darkness, and she saw the goodness in every person.

Mama was 91 years old when she died. Our daughter Lynn had been trying to conceive a child for some time, and right around the time of mother's death she became pregnant with her son Sky. We cannot help but feel their souls are intertwined—that our grandson is mama's gift to us.

I WISH I COULD SAY ALL OF HAWAII'S PROBLEMS were solved. In fact I left office troubled by problems in several areas, some of which remain with me to this day. One is the functioning of higher education in Hawaii—a subject of intense concern to people everywhere. During the time Jack Burns was governor, there was a euphoria and idealism about the University of Hawaii. Dr. Thomas H. Hamilton came in as president and gave us strong leadership. When Harlan Cleveland came in as president, the university was permitted to function and grow more or less on its own. In my view the growth was propelled mainly by student desires to get involved in this or that program, rather than by a community-based vision. As a result of people applying for graduate degrees, and developing programs of graduate study, there was a time when 270 advanced degrees were being granted by UH. This was costly and disjointed.

When Dr. Fujio Matsuda became president in 1974, he was cognizant of this problem. He tried to pull back in some areas, set priorities, and determine what kind of university we really ought to have. He understood that this university, on this island, in the middle of the Pacific, supported by a small state with limited resources, could not have excellent programs in everything. To achieve excellence, we had to focus on areas in which we could genuinely excel. Dr. Matsuda's thinking was on the right track, but he had a hard time getting support at the university for his ideas. The faculty was entrenched. The programs were entrenched. Nobody wanted to give in. By 1984, with Dr. Matsuda headed for retirement, I was aware of time passing in the last term of my governorship and of my continuing frustration. I agreed with Dr. Matsuda's thinking and felt he had developed strategic plans that needed and deserved additional support. I was determined that I would pursue the direction laid out by him.

I set aside twelve afternoons and told the university to arrange my itinerary for outings to the Manoa campus. I would spend an entire afternoon with a single college. The first hour was with the department head. Then I would meet with the faculty. I wanted to know how the university people looked at themselves, at me, and at the State Administration in general. What I got from them was intense frustration about their inability to achieve operational results, which they felt they had a right to. They were blaming me, along with the Department of Budget and Finance and the Department of Accounting and General Services.

In many instances I felt the types of problems they cited were not our fault, but rather were problems coming from within the university. In response, I tried to meet everyone halfway and create a working strategy for getting a new definition of the university on track. "But," I said, "we ought to focus more on the nature of the university, and develop priorities. We ought to answer the question, 'In what ways can we achieve excellence?' This place—Hawaii, what kind of place can it be? What can you do to take it there? In what areas can we truly be the very best in the world, because of our location, our people, our ethnic mix, and the cultural understanding of our community?'"

Dr. Matsuda's plans revolved around environmentally related sciences in which our ecosystem and location give us a special advantage (for example, in marine biology, ocean science, alternate energy, astronomy, and tropical agriculture). I came to believe we should also make a bid for leadership in the social sciences, based on the idea of Hawaii as a "mixing pot." I fervently hoped that Dr. Matsuda's successor, by starting out with these ideas in hand, could put them into action.

After a confusing search process, the new president turned out to be the acting president, Dr. Albert Simone. I called him in one day and told him about my experiences with the university people. I told him my vision for the university. I told him I wanted him to be a strong president, and to support him I would meet everyone at least halfway. I said, "I want to give you strength on campus by bringing about changes that the faculty wants. Go back to the Faculty Senate. Tell them to give you a list of what needs to be changed so the university has more autonomy."

He came back to me with a list. He said he didn't expect me to grant it all but he felt he should at least present it to me. I looked at the list and said, "Dr. Simone, I'll give you all of this, plus some things you haven't asked me for."

I said, "Please feel free to tell everyone you convinced me these were the things that had to be done for the university to have real autonomy. In return, the faculty owes something to the community and to the State. I want them to take responsibility for putting together a plan that would make our university one of excellence."

I told Dr. Simone I would go to campus and make the announcement if he so desired. I said, "With this, the faculty should support you in moving the university in the direction we should be moving—not being everything to everybody, but truly excellent in some carefully chosen fields."

I went to the campus and talked about ways the university would be given greater autonomy. My remarks were well received, and everyone was happy. I introduced several bills into the Legislature clarifying the nature of the university's operational and academic autonomy. These passed.

However, I never saw the rest of it. I did not feel that we were given the kind of response I wanted. I was left with the feeling that the university still must ask itself, "What kind of university are we going to have? In what areas can we find excellence?" A governor cannot impose that. At least part of the vision must be generated by the university community coming together and developing it themselves. I didn't get that back then, and I don't see it happening now.

As a result of such experiences, the general community that supports the Manoa campus continues to have an uneasy relationship with it. I belabor this point because currently our students are worried about whether they can get the courses they need, whether they can secure a good degree, and whether they then can go on to graduate schools. Despite pressures on the budget, students should not have to worry about such things. They should know we will *always* have a strong liberal arts program, because any really good university must have liberal arts as the base from which students can specialize. We should get grounded in this concept and look for cuts in the many graduate programs if they are necessary.

A keener, more active awareness of community needs would help this situation. Recently the government recruited teachers on the Mainland in response to a large number of teachers retiring. This occurred in the context of young people in Hawaii needing gratifying work, and also in the context of minority groups complaining about lack of representation in the ranks of teachers. Why had we not trained more teachers? Comparable situations still occur in public health programs—we recruit people from the Mainland when we should be filling these positions with people who have been educated in Hawaii and are highly sensitized to the cultural complexities of Hawaii. These are basics.

On a more visionary level, we must again undertake our drive to create a university that excels. We should start with the core idea of Hawaii as a "mixing pot," where each of us retains our own identity but comes together with others for our mutual cultural enrichment. We are a stew. We get tastier but we don't melt down. Using this "mixing pot" metaphor, we can be a leader in teaching people how to work together. We can lead in the social sciences that have to do with human and cross-cultural interaction. It is ironic, and also instructive, that we already are recognized for our strengths in Asian and Pacific studies, such as Japanese Studies, Chinese Studies, Korean Studies and Philippine Studies. We have Hawaiian Studies and Ethnic Studies but the next step —how these elements come together—is missing. I think it is because a working concept of the "mixing pot" is missing.

If we look at how far we are from any other state, and truly grasp the significance of being the only island state in America, we will generate a sense of mission for the university that is unique but fits in a national and international context. In the sciences, alternate energy development is a prime example of a priority program. There are many others, such as ocean-based aquaculture or mariculture, which can provide answers to issues of world food supply as world population grows and conventional resources are exhausted.

To achieve our potential, we must identify what makes us different, embrace it, and make it work for us. We must seize the advantages of being separate, and of pursuing the possibilities that are unique to us. If we do not see how different we are, we will drift toward outward sameness, yet we will never be a contiguous part of the United States. We will never enjoy the advantages of being an integral part of a continent.

This idea of a unique mission for the university was essentially what I would have liked to have gotten across as governor, but that does not mean that we can give up. The situation is there, the challenge is there, and the opportunities are there as well.

DURING MY TIME AS GOVERNOR I was confronted with two intensely emotional controversies that bordered on hysteria. They led me to realize there are times of intense public feeling when you not only have to do the right thing, but you have to be seen as doing the right thing—and not for narrow personal or political advantage, but for the general public's well-being. One situation was the leaching of a chemical known as PPCD through the soil and into the underground water sources beneath the Central Oahu plain. The second was the passage of a chemical known as heptachlor through pineapple "chop," or tops and leaves, into the feed of dairy cattle, and from there into the milk supply.

In both instances, traces of cancer-causing substances were detected. As governor it was my job to balance the risk against the range of effects resulting from remedial action. On the extreme end of the PPCD case, I was practically urged to shut down the sugar industry. But in carefully consulting the available experts, and in carefully weighing the evidence, the risk appeared negligible. Nothing is absolutely pure, nor absolutely without risk. Against this almost indecipherable risk, I needed to consider the huge impact on our community if sugar were shut down—not only questions of the economy and people's livelihood, but questions of land use and the temptation that would arise to develop the idle lands. By way of remediating the PPCD situation, I shut down wells. Systems of filtration were installed in some of the wells. But nonetheless I was severely criticized.

In the heptachlor situation, I again got every possible assurance from a range of medical experts, but that nagging doubt still persisted. Lay people still said, "You can't really be sure until fifteen or twenty years have gone by." Almost by definition, that is true, but now that much time actually has passed, and there is no evidence or pattern of environmentally caused disease. The dire predictions have not come to pass. After all these years, I am convinced I handled these situations correctly. I am reinforced in my belief that I listened to the right experts and properly weighed the right set of evidence. I didn't panic. However, I am still burdened by the fact that I was unable to adequately communicate the facts of these situations to the general public. I failed to allay peoples' widespread fears.

PERHAPS NOTHING HAS SO NEGATIVELY AFFECTED the quality of public life as the large sums of money spent on campaigning. It occurs in context of the fact that our community ties have been weakened by the growth of the population, and by the impact of television. TV encourages people to sit at home rather than getting involved with their neighbors. Where the old-fashioned campaign rally was a "free medium" for us as young candidates, today there is no equivalent.

We currently have an elaborate system of soliciting campaign money through the sale of tickets to fund-raising get-togethers. Everybody who appears before the Legislature is asked to buy tickets to fund-raisers. Supporters of candidates are besieged to buy tickets. Informally there is a master calendar of fund-raisers circulated within the Legislature to minimize scheduling conflicts, which should tell us something about how elaborate the fund-raising system has become.

In many races, actual expenditures far exceed what the ordinary person would think of as reasonable. Geographically, State House districts today are quite small, because they are single-member districts. Where I was one of six people elected to represent the sprawling Fifth House District in 1954, only one person represents a district today. There are twenty-two districts inside the old Fifth House Districts as it existed when I first ran. As a result of the small size of districts, candidates can make personal contact with a large percentage of all voters. This should alleviate the need to spend large amounts of money, since mass media is the most important cost element of campaigns, yet expenditures within these small districts are enormous. Running in 1954 in a Territorial House district that covered over four-fifths of the geographic area of Oahu, I spent five hundred dollars or thereabouts. Recently one candidate spent several hundred times that amount in a small, single-member district on a losing campaign. Two years later, this same candidate spent an equivalent amount in the same small district and won.

I didn't even have a finance committee for my first seventeen election campaigns, until I ran for lieutenant governor. In contrast, financial backing is often the first thing a young candidate thinks of.

Although some individuals' practices are more aggressive than others, the ills of the campaign finance system affect everyone. By the time I got into statewide races, television was a big factor in determining the success of a campaign. Huge sums of money were spent on my behalf, as well as on campaigns to defeat me. I never liked it. I was never comfortable with it. When I was lieutenant governor, a law was developed in the Legislature setting limits on spending, but within a few years it was declared an unconstitutional violation of free speech. The courts translated the First Amendment to mean a candidate must be free to spend as much money as he or she likes. While we can restrict the amounts given, we cannot restrict the amount spent. Subsequently the Legislature has tried to offset the effect of money in campaigns by the establishment of a Campaign Spending Commission, by disclosure of contributions, by prohibitions on the size of contributions, and so on. These ideas have not worked effectively. In the 1994 gubernatorial campaign, the three major candidates spent a combined total of well over $9 million, a staggering sum of money.

In rethinking campaign financing, the public must look at itself as well. Community groups continuously ask legislators to fund charitable events, sponsor athletic teams, or otherwise assist with grassroots fundraising events. The money comes from campaign accounts, and it adds up.

To deal with the corrosive effect of the campaign financing system, we must return to the idea of setting absolute limits on expenditures. I know there have been constitutional problems with this idea, but times change. So much money is spent today, and the effect on the public trust is so corrosive, that we must again tackle the constitutional question. We can only hope that, with the passage of time and the obvious failure of lesser reforms, the attitude of the court will change.

As I pursued the idea of showcasing Hawaii's unique assets, my Administration turned to the possibilities of Honolulu's waterfront. In the process we laid groundwork for redevelopment of the Honolulu harbor area, but as part of that I felt strongly we should have an International Trade Center at the harbor's traditional landmark, Aloha Tower. The idea was to locate international businesses there with the latest support services and infrastructure in the realms of communication and technology. I was unable to sell the idea.

I experienced a similar frustration over the concept of an Ocean Center, which was to have been designed to reflect our ocean heritage and spur wise and creative use of ocean resources. It also was to have been a first-rate aquarium and a source of enjoyment for visitor and resident alike. I envisioned connecting the Ocean Center by hydrofoil to other stops along the waterfront, including the International Trade Center. Existing interests were disturbed, and the consensus I sought to develop eluded me.

As you have seen by now, my wife Jeannie and I are close. I always kept her well informed. She knew why I was doing what I was doing, and we maintained a deep sense of understanding and balance. We worked together to help the children be part of the process, and to understand the facts when things were said against us. Jeannie carried the brunt of this effort.

She let me be governor and never interfered with the decisions that I had to make. She was always supportive. During campaigns the family was solidly committed, and they were comfortable coming out with me to campaign events. Jeannie went with me to coffee hours. She also went to many coffee hours on her own and spoke for me. Often these were swings through the Neighbor Islands when I was not available to go, which meant that she carried the campaign solely on her own shoulders. She took a low-key approach, meeting groups for coffee and conversation, getting acquainted and making friends but typically not talking politics. She met so many people and developed so many good relationships that when I would go to Hawaii, Maui, or Kauai, people would ask, "Where is Jeannie?" I think they were coming out to see her instead of me.

As first lady, she was heavily involved in charitable and community causes. She began by visiting every free lunch center with a group of volunteer Hawaiian musicians. Then she led a group of ten volunteers to work regularly with patients at State Hospital. She worked with senior citizens and shut-ins as well. Finally she sat down with the State Volunteer Services Program and devised a recognition program to boost the morale and visibility of volunteers. It was called the First Lady's Volunteer Award, and the annual ceremonies on each island grew, over eleven years, from involving a handful of people to well over a thousand. A blue-ribbon committee selected the outstanding volunteer in five categories: Youth, adult, senior citizen, organization, and projects.[23]

I think Jean's most special mission was working on the history of Washington Place. She read extensively and talked with people about Queen Lili'uokalani, whose home it had been. She became knowledgeable about the life of the queen, as well as the art and furnishings of the place and the time period. People would call her and say they had items that had belonged to the queen. In some instances the pieces were authenticated, and some of the queen's possessions were returned to Washington Place as a result. A university class joined in some of the more laborious tasks, such as making pencil-rubbings of the bottoms of chairs and tables as a means of cataloguing them. An investigative or research phase went on for six years, and with the help of Dr. Mary Elle Des Jarlais she published her findings in a limited edition, *Decorative Arts of Washington Place 1847-1987*, for others to review.

Jean directed restoration work on Washington Place for another four years. She also worked out a way to open Washington Place to public visits. To manage public access, she trained a group of docents who became highly conversant on the objects and the history. She personally gave tours of the house to the extent that she could, and she particularly enjoyed having children come through. Washington Place was open to the public as never before.

One night the native Hawaiian leader A. "Frenchy" DeSoto was at Washington Place. Jean took her through the house, and then Frenchy asked to spend a little time alone in the queen's bedroom. When she came out she had tears in her eyes. She said she was so pleased that a Japanese girl had taken care of the heritage of Hawaiians, and she gave Jeannie a big hug.

Another night, one of the respected Hawaiian societies, the Daughters and Sons of Hawaiian Warriors, visited with Jean at Washington Place. As an expression of their appreciation for the care and respect given to Washington Place, and generally for her interest in Hawaiian history and culture, the women of the society wanted to honor Jean with a gift. They gathered in their black holoku gowns and chanted, revealing the name they had decided upon for Jean—Kaleinanioka'aina, which means the beautiful lady of the land. She felt it was one of the most touching moments of her life.

[23]The program was continued by Jean's successor, Lynne Waihee.

During the gubernatorial campaign of 1994, Ben Cayetano announced that he would return Washington Place to the native Hawaiian people. He made this announcement as a symbol of his support for restoring sovereignty to the Hawaiians, but Jean thought it was a premature idea. She as well as anyone understood the complexity of maintaining the house, its limits as a museum, the way that it supports a governor in logistic and security terms, etc. As the place to gather and host people, it says eloquently that Hawaii once was an independent nation and that we have a unique past and a unique role in the world. After Cayetano was elected, Jean wrote him a letter, and it apparently contributed to his rethinking his position.

IN 1985, HAWAII PREPARED TO CELEBRATE the hundredth anniversary of the *Kanyaku Imin*—the first well-organized arrival of contract workers from Japan. Jeannie told me the celebration would be more meaningful if we left something behind. She said she wanted to have five million trees planted. I gulped and then she said, "Well, maybe *one* million trees for the million residents of Hawaii." I told her that meant a thousand groups planting at least a thousand trees apiece, but as a mathematician she obviously knew that. She worked with many volunteer organizations and they ended up planting 1,168,000 trees.[24] Not only were the trees planted, but people came to a greater appreciation of trees and how to care for them.

---

[24]The co-chair was John "Doc" Buyers, the president of C. Brewer and chairman of the Hawaiian Sugar Planters Association, which was celebrating its 150th anniversary in the year of the *Kanyaku Imin*.

*(Top) Jean's most special mission was the history
of Washington Place. Here she is seated at the piano
of Queen Liliʻuokalani.*

*(Bottom) My mother and daughter Lynn greet me
as I go to take the oath of office.*

(Following page) My election gave pride to many people.

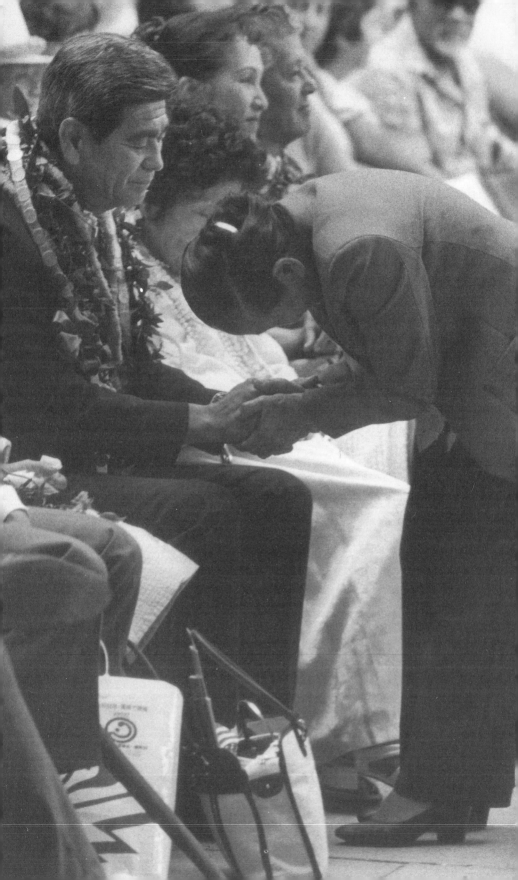

CHAPTER TWELVE

Being Who We Are

IN MY 1979 STATE OF THE STATE ADDRESS, I said: "Hawaii has stood for many years as a beacon of light in a world darkened by bigotry—not a perfect beacon, to be sure, but one which shines more clearly than in any other place on earth." Our beacon of light represents "what the entire world must increasingly come to know, and to understand, and to practice."

My job as governor was to move the practice of equality and equal opportunity forward. This task, which all of us share, has two aspects. One is to prove the perpetrators of racial stereotypes to be wrong. The other is to help the victims of prejudice heal themselves.

I was personally aware of traces of prejudice. When I was elected there were still people who were very much against having a person of Japanese ancestry become governor. I used to get mail saying, "Don't forget this is America," or, "You damn Jap." Some of it was signed and some not. The mail started at the beginning of my term and continued. There was not a lot, but it kept coming. Some of it seemed to be prompted by my proposals to control growth, as if I had introduced an alien concept.

I never responded. One person wrote me nasty letters repeatedly, and I ignored him completely. At one point, he indicated he wanted to come in and see me. I did not want to meet with such a person, because I couldn't have listened with any sense that what he said had any validity.

I didn't let the mail bother me, because I didn't want to let it affect the way I governed. I never let this mail be publicized. My father always told me that to accomplish your work, you have to be positive. Arguing, bickering, and being negative don't do anything for you. A positive person makes things happen. I didn't want anybody to diminish my positive attitude.

What I did try to do was demonstrate that whether I was Japanese or Chinese or Hawaiian or Caucasian didn't make any difference, that I was governor of all the people.

The mere fact of a non-white person being elected governor expanded many people's horizons. When schoolchildren came to see me, they often wanted to take pictures. I would have one of the youngsters come sit in my chair, and I'd tell the child, "*You* can become governor."

Governor Burns, in one of his most famous phrases, alluded to a "subtle inferiority of spirit" afflicting some of our people, a sense that was totally unwarranted and that had to be discarded once and for all. I felt I knew what he meant. For decades we had been barraged with messages, some blatant and some subtle, that we could go only so far, that we were different, that somehow we had to change in order to fit in.

These things hurt. They create wounds that need to be healed by a change in practice and a change in mentality.

A variation of the old messages occurred around the time I came home from law school. Again, we were confronted with the issue of how to be ourselves—and to be proud of it. There was a lot of talk about eliminating the various ethnic chambers of commerce. The idea was that we shouldn't have a Chinese Chamber of Commerce, or a Japanese Chamber of Commerce. In the new day that was then dawning, some people seemed to be saying that to be a good American was to forget your own background.

I did not think that was a good idea. I began to reflect critically on the words "melting pot." I wondered whether that was the right description of what Hawaii should be. While it was true we were all thrown into the same pot and stirred up together, should we all come out tasting the same? I inclined toward the idea that each of us adds something to the stew, hence my use of the words "mixing pot." To be proud of what you are is to be a self-confident contributor to the whole. To be proud of what you are is to be ready to reach out, dream, and achieve.

A governor has the opportunity, and also the responsibility, to attend many community events and to socialize with widely varying people. I often saw different ethnic groups give cultural presentations in settings of their own making. Sometimes they were Japanese or Okinawan, Korean, Filipino, Hawaiian or Vietnamese, down to some very small groups who —despite their small numbers—maintain vibrant cultural traditions in Hawaii. I spent a lot of time watching not only the performances but how the audiences responded. I could see the gleam in people's eyes when their traditions were celebrated. I sought, in every way I could, to infuse that pride not only into people's special celebrations but into their everyday lives.

One day I was on Maui speaking to a group of community college students. I gave them my thoughts and feelings. Afterwards two girls of Filipino ancestry came up to me, and we talked a little while. They told me they sometimes felt inferior—they sometimes felt a little ashamed of their own cultural background and wanted to be something other than what they were.

I told them, "Don't feel like that! You're as good as anybody else. You can achieve as much as anybody else. Don't hold yourself back by being ashamed, because you will become less of a person. If you ever buy into the idea that you're inferior to someone else, you can never reach your potential. You'll put a limit on what you can become. You can never reach out for that higher level of achievement. You can never really dream. You don't have to become someone else to be as good as someone else. Be yourself. Be proud of who you are." I remember this one girl's face in particular, because she began to cry.

Regardless of what we do, most of us tend to think big thoughts in youth and to narrow our focus during the hard work of middle age. Being governor allowed me to revisit the ideas I had as a young man and to share them with others. As this went on, I acquired a growing conviction that by truly being who we are, we really are helping not only ourselves but others. We can set an example for others. Perhaps we can help other people overcome whatever vestiges of prejudice they are carrying around. We can broaden and enrich their outlook and understanding.

As governor, I had many occasions to use my understanding of the Japanese language. I spoke with pride about the values embedded in the words and phrases my father had taught me. I sometimes conversed in Japanese. On a few occasions I delivered speeches in Japanese. Some people said that because I was an American governor, "not a Japanese governor," I should not do this. Within the Japan Hawaii Economic Council, which I helped form, I sometimes spoke to the Japanese delegation in their language, ignoring the translation process. I was practically alone among the Americans in my understanding of Japanese, and I was told that some of my fellow Americans found my Japanese irritating. Perhaps people who thought in "us" versus "them" terms wondered, which side was I on?

My response to the critics is essentially, "What does it take to be an American? What is an American? Who is an American? Does an American have narrow views? Or does an American not only tolerate but understand many points of view and many different backgrounds and cultures?"

IN 1962, EIGHT YEARS AFTER I FIRST HAD RUN for office, I was approached to sit on the board of the First Hawaiian Bank. The bank was founded by Charles Reed Bishop, husband of Princess Pauahi Bishop. It is one of Hawaii's two largest banks. Historically it had been very much a part of the old oligarchic structure, which made the invitation to join their board of directors intriguing. It was apparent that the process of change was reaching into the economic realm, because about this time the renowned attorney (later Supreme Court justice) Masaji Marumoto was asked to be on the board of First Hawaiian Bank's competitor, the Bank of Hawaii.

My first response was, "I'm a Democrat. I can't sit on a big bank's board of directors." Then I thought about the reasons for my getting involved in politics. I thought, "Here is an opportunity to help open things up. If I say no to them, then in a small way I'm going to make it more difficult for the openness I seek to come about." It was an opportunity for me to work within the system to bring about some of the changes that we Democrats had sought.

After I got on the board, the president of the bank came to me. He said they didn't have anybody to take over a key middle management position. They would have to go outside of Hawaii to find the person, to Seattle, or San Francisco, or other traditional recruiting grounds for Hawaii executives. My response to this was, "I would be embarrassed if I were in your situation to have to admit that I don't have, amongst all of the employees that I have, anybody who dreamed of advancing up the ranks and preparing themselves for it."

I told the bank president we should have ten or fifteen people who were so qualified that he would have a wide field of choices from within the ranks. I told him the bank, for so long, had conveyed to people they wouldn't advance that they no longer dared to dream, they didn't strive, they didn't work themselves up. They had stopped trying to advance, and they had stopped learning. They became interested in only doing their existing tasks with blinders on, and doing no more than they were required.

I urged the bank to create an executive training program through which people could stir themselves, be challenged, make a greater contribution and compete for the executive jobs. I promised the bank president that if the bank promoted from within wherever possible, he would have many people ready to take these jobs.

Subsequently I had the privilege of voting to make the part-Hawaiian Johnny Bellinger the president of the bank. Johnny Bellinger worked his way up from bank clerk. He became a legend in banking and community circles and well-known throughout the Pacific and in Japan. He was a great businessman and an outstanding human being. I liked him because he never forgot where he came from, and he would often reach back and help others along the path.

It may surprise you to know I continued to fight such battles within the State bureaucracy throughout my governorship. I particularly remember people at the University of Hawaii saying they couldn't find qualified administrators in Hawaii, and the only possible solution was to go to the Mainland. I told them to look harder. I admit there were times when you need to shake things up by bringing someone in, or look outside for someone with an extremely rare set of skills, but the general rule for any self-respecting locale should be to develop its own talents and put them to work.

I believe that in Hawaii during the 1960s, 1970s, and 1980s, we progressed to the point where I felt I could tell anyone and everyone with conviction, "Your possibilities are limited only by your hard work and desire." As I write in the mid-1990s, I am no longer so sure this is true. The battles Jack Burns fought, and that I fought, still go on today in different ways. Our economy has progressively become part of the national and then global economy. Many of the companies that have come into Hawaii have not gone through the education of getting acquainted with our multicultural people. I think some companies exhibit a sense of condescension that takes us backward rather than forward. To give them the benefit of the doubt, their behavior may be unconscious, but it is destructive nonetheless.

RELATIONS AMONG HAWAII'S DIVERSE PEOPLE are further complicated today by the broadly based movement among native Hawaiians to achieve some form of sovereignty. Some people find this movement a cause for optimism which, at best, will result in a resolution or healing of native issues that have clouded our history ever since the overthrow of Queen Lili'uokalani. Others find this movement confusing and dismaying.

Much of the Democratic Party's history in Hawaii revolved around achieving truly first-class citizenship, which meant becoming full participants in the American experience. As part of this effort, native Hawaiians were very much a part of the Democratic Party. A core of native Hawaiians were in on the founding of the Democratic Party, and they helped keep the Democratic Party going in the politically bleak years before the 1954 election. Honolulu Mayor Johnny Wilson, a Hawaiian, was probably the most prominent Democrat in the pre-1954 period. He gave voice to the downtrodden and also nurtured those who had the courage to buck the old system.

The Hawaiian agenda has changed and evolved. During my tenure as governor, I addressed the long-standing frustration with the Hawaiian Homes program by putting approximately $50 million from the State treasury into creating infrastructure for new homesteads. This doubled the number of Hawaiian families in the program. We put more people into homes during my time in office than had occurred in the preceding five decades, although there always were those who were quick to say it was too little, too late.[25]

I was also the first governor to recognize that the State of Hawaii's Executive Orders appropriating Hawaiian Homes Lands for State use should not continue. I canceled all State Executive Orders that had been issued before my time in office. The land was either returned to the Department of Hawaiian Homes Lands or the terms were renegotiated. In some instances, such as the airport property, we negotiated and bought the property.

During the 1970s, the climate of Hawaiian community life changed rapidly, as Hawaiians took a renewed interest in their culture, history, and language. Native Hawaiians began to reaffirm and reassert themselves. These changes came into focus at the 1978 Constitutional Convention. A set of amendments was developed that acknowledged the special status of native Hawaiians as indigenous people. The Hawaiian language was established as the official language of the State of Hawaii, along with English. Another amendment outlined native rights. A third created the Office of Hawaiian Affairs (OHA). I supported ratification of the work of the Constitutional Convention, and after the public officially adopted the changes, I worked with the State Legislature on implementation. I was sympathetic with OHA when they had growing pains, and I tried to tell people, "Look, they're in an infancy stage, and there are issues they need to work out themselves. Let them grow." I also went along with turning over some of the income from the ceded lands trust to OHA.

I think progress has been made, but that is not the focus of community discussion today. The focus is on the historic grievance of native Hawaiians, and what is wrong. People say, "Hawaiians have the highest school dropout rates, the highest rates of people in prison, the highest

---

[25]I often had heard of native Hawaiians being frustrated with the length of the waiting list. I learned that the individuals are often not ready to actually make the move. We went through five names on the list to get one person and their family moved into a home.

numbers of people on welfare, and so on." As governor, I badly wanted to nurture the development of Hawaiian entrepreneurs, so people would say, "We have Hawaiian businesses. If they can make it, I can make it. My kids can make it." I wanted OHA, the Department of Hawaiian Homes Lands, and Alu Like (a native training and education program) to work together on creating a native Hawaiian enterprise center. I set aside a prime place, Pohukaina School, in the State-controlled redevelopment area of Kakaako, just below downtown, for this purpose. I was disappointed this business-oriented initiative fell by the way after I left office. It had such a potential for creating a more positive climate.

I share the historical view that an injustice was done. A wrong was committed, and Hawaiians are entitled to redress. That redress must not come only from the people of Hawaii, but it must be a national effort. The issues of sovereignty have to do with the circumstances of the overthrow of the monarchy and annexation to the United States, and therefore have to do with the relationship of native Hawaiians to the American nation.

In the process of resolving the issue of sovereignty, we must remember that many generations of Westerners and Asians have put down their roots in Hawaii. Many people have intermarried with native Hawaiians. The rest of the people in Hawaii today, who are not native Hawaiians, are also deserving of a place under the sun.

(Above)
Jean and I meet Deng Xiaoping.

(Opposite page)
My mother greets Emperor Hirohito at Washington Place,
along with my sons Ryozo and Donn.
I represented the United States at the funeral of Japanese Prime Minister Masayoshi Ohira,
along with Mike Mansfield, then ambassador to Japan (to my right),
and (to his right) Secretary of State Edmund Muskie and President Jimmy Carter.

(Following pages)
The arrival of the British royal family was a test of my belief
in the importance of simply being oneself.
I was honored to be the recipient of the Grand Cordon of the Sacred Treasure
from the government of my parents' homeland.

CHAPTER THIRTEEN
Hawaii and the Pacific

THE PROGRESS WE MAKE RESOLVING ETHNIC and racial issues of life in Hawaii is interrelated with our stepping out in the world to become a participant in international life. I had a special experience in Japan that I think sheds light on this point. While I was governor I was invited to speak at an event in Tokyo organized by the Japanese government. The focus was on groups who had emigrated from Japan to Hawaii, the U.S. Mainland and South America. Mingling in the crowd prior to the formal gathering, I met a person of Japanese ancestry from Brazil. I asked what generation of Japanese he was in Brazil.

He told me, "I am Brazilian."

I told him, "But aren't you also Japanese?"

He told me, "No, I am Brazilian."

He steadfastly refused to acknowledge he was originally from Japan, or his parents, or whoever it had been. I asked someone else about his background and was told that a number of Brazilians had a rough, rough time during World War II. They were picked on and ostracized to the point where they tried to hide the fact that their ancestry was Japanese. Subsequently they could not overcome this mentality of denial. In constantly reciting their claim to being Brazilian, they no longer admitted to their Japanese ancestry. This man had a Japanese face that was unmistakable and inescapable. I was personally troubled by my exchange with him. Perhaps it was because his experience was an exaggerated version of what we had been through in Hawaii.

I was to be one of four speakers to a group of several hundred that included Shintaro Abe, who then was the foreign minister of Japan, as well as Crown Prince Akihito and Princess Michiko, his wife, later the Emperor and Empress of Japan. The other three speakers were to speak in Japanese, but I had been asked to prepare my remarks in English for translation into Japanese. Particular attention was given to form and protocol because of the presence of the then Crown Prince and Princess. But on the spur of the moment, in response to my new acquaintance from Brazil, I told my translator to please forget what she had worked on, because I was going to speak in Japanese. While I was uncomfortable with the quality of my Japanese, particularly in context of people of high rank in Japan, I nonetheless was proud of the Japanese I did speak.

I discarded my English text and began to speak extemporaneously. After asking everyone to forgive my poor Japanese, I told about the time right after the war when I first had come to Japan as part of the occupation force. I had come to a devastated society. Food was scarce. The buildings were destroyed. The economy was in ruins. The U.S. military was in total control. When I returned to Japan, I saw the miracle of the economic recovery that had taken place in such a short period of time. I kept asking myself how this had happened. I thought about the fact that energy sources and most raw materials were imported, about the work force and domestic market being just half the size of the United States, about the fact—as Ambassador Mike Mansfield often said—that all of the land mass of this island nation would fit inside his home state of Montana. How could a country under those circumstances develop so quickly into such a great economic power?

I said the United States had assisted with support and encouragement, but the most essential ingredients had come from within Japan— the hard work, spirit, and the willingness of the people to look to the future and say, "No matter how much I suffer I want the future to be better. I want my children to have a better future," or *kodomo no tame ni,* for the sake of the children, as the first generation in Hawaii had said.

As I spoke, I increasingly focused my attention on where the Brazilian man was sitting. In my mind I was speaking directly to him. I said how proud I was to trace my roots to such a strong cultural tradition. I said this tradition had sustained my parents in Hawaii, helping them to overcome great difficulties and to participate in the creation of a modern, progressive society. "All of us can feel that in the future no matter what happens, and no matter where we go, we can overcome extreme obstacles," I said. "That is the lesson of the past—that none of us should hold ourselves back. None of us need be ashamed of saying who we are, what we are, or where we've come from. We can take off the shackles of the past, and we can reach out and dream."

I looked again at this person of Japanese ancestry from Brazil. There were tears in his eyes. Prince Akihito was sitting on stage behind me. Jean said he kept looking at me as if he were trying to tell whether I was reading a text or speaking off the cuff. Thereafter he and the empress always graciously remembered me. Jean and I were invited to the funeral ceremony—called *taiso no rei*—of his father, the Emperor Hirohito.

Subsequently we were among the five hundred foreign citizens invited to his enthronement ceremony, which is called *sokui no rei*. Most of the people there were heads of state or royalty. I was not only a commoner, but by then I was a former governor, albeit of a special American state. When the emperor and empress came to America in 1994, Jean and I were among the hundred guests invited by President Clinton to the State dinner at the White House. A few days later I delivered the formal greeting to the emperor and empress at the Japanese consulate reception in Honolulu.

JAPAN TAKES A KEEN INTEREST IN THE EXPERIENCE that people of Japanese ancestry have in America. Because of this, Japan is extraordinarily conscious of Hawaii. For my part, I experienced moments in Japan that were quite special to me. I felt I was spanning the immigrant generation and the new American generation, and also spanning the historic distance between our two countries.

Early in my governorship, the Japanese government in conjunction with the National Governors Association of Japan hosted me on a tour, prominently including southwestern Japan, from where my parents had emigrated. My mother, Jean, and I visited Kumamoto Prefecture, where Mother was born. We also visited Fukuoka Prefecture, where Papa was born. In Fukuoka, we were taken to a school in a small village. They showed us my father's third-grade class picture and his report card. His marks were excellent. Because the third grade was his last year in school, I was amazed all over again at the opportunities he had given me.

It must have been there, in the small village, that he learned the *sumo* that he brought with him to Hawaii. I still have his ceremonial *sumo* apron, which in Japanese is called a *kesho mawashi*. It is a beautiful *kesho mawashi* made of white and gold embroidery and braids.

WHILE MOMENTS SUCH AS BEING IN PAPA'S VILLAGE were important to me personally, I would never have experienced them if I had not been governor of Hawaii, so it is in that particular light that I want to share some of my Pacific stories.

Recently a newspaper editor posed the question: Is Hawaii in the center of the Pacific or the middle of nowhere? Geographically, our Islands are farther from other land masses than any other islands on earth. Literally, we are the most remote islands on the planet, which is why Darwin wanted to study the differentiation of species in Hawaii. We are the only American island state, located nearly halfway to Japan.

Our people are all sojourners from around the Pacific—some from ancient times, some from the nineteenth century, some quite recently. We have an international tradition that goes back more than a century. Our internationalism has nurtured a unique in-migration, resulting in the establishment of important international institutions, the most visible of which is the East-West Center.

Our tradition of internationalism co-exists with a streak of parochialism. Many of us in Hawaii tend to feel we have "arrived," that we are at the center of the universe, and everything is arrayed around us. Many of us have turned inward, to our detriment. Are we international or parochial? Are we in the center of the Pacific or the middle of nowhere? I believe that successfully resolving this division within ourselves is at the heart of our future. The outcome will affect economic growth, education, and opportunity in a broad sense.

The more we get out in the world, the more clearly we can see what is distinctive about Hawaii. The more we appreciate others, the more we appreciate ourselves. Since the early 1970s, I have been immersed in developing relationships for Hawaii around the Pacific. As lieutenant governor I was a founding member of the Japan-Hawaii Economic Council. I was involved in stimulating Asian travel to Hawaii. These efforts—undertaken in concert with many other people—were overwhelmingly successful. The success story of the Japan relationship needs little elaboration for anyone who lives in Hawaii, travels here, or does business here. Japan is our most important relationship but far from our only one. We have many less visible relationships with other countries and other islands of the Pacific. We need to nurture these other relationships just as we have nurtured our relationship with Japan. If we manage them with sensitivity and common sense, we will benefit immensely.

To GENUINELY PARTICIPATE IN THE PACIFIC AGE, we have to begin by effectively working with other islands in the Pacific. In my capacity as governor, I struck up friendships with the governors of the American territories in the Pacific, the so-called American Flag Pacific Islands, consisting of Guam, American Samoa, and the Commonwealth of the Northern Marianas Islands. These island territories are under the administrative jurisdiction of the U.S. Department of the Interior. The governors of these island territories often came through Hawaii on their way to either the National Governors Association or the Western Governors Conference.

As we talked, I realized they often felt isolated, voiceless, and powerless. As our acquaintances grew, they became outspoken in their criticism of the Federal government. They complained that the Federal government was insensitive to their needs and sometimes outright uncaring. I was inclined to be sympathetic, because that was how the Federal government dealt with Hawaii when we were a territory. The agenda of the forty-nine continental states (or forty-eight contiguous states) oftentimes had no bearing on the lives of Islanders, and sometimes none on the lives of the people of Hawaii—such as discussions of interstate highway maintenance, river traffic, the management of regional watersheds, regional mining, the management of regional forests, etc. For some of the same reasons, Hawaii occasionally had interests that were shared primarily with the American Flag islands, such as the regulation of the migratory tuna within the irregular 200-mile limit of islands.

Sometimes I outlined the concerns of the American Flag governors to the U. S. Interior Department. Sometimes I argued their case. On a couple of occasions I critiqued the attitudes of Interior Department executives, insisting they take island problems more seriously. I alerted our congressional delegation to issues they should watch for and push on. In this regard I should note that our delegation was responsive and had relationships in the Pacific that predated my own. We helped the territories with Federal aid to education, social services, health care, economic development, and so on. The American Flag governors and I progressed from meeting in Honolulu to meeting just after the governors' conferences, wherever a conference was held. By 1980, we had reached a point of proposing that the Pacific Island governors, including Hawaii's, have our own governors' organization, to be called the Pacific Basin Development Council. Agreement was reached, and we began twice-yearly meetings with systematic staff support, headquartered in Honolulu.

This work reinforced my deep sense of island people being culturally distinct. They are more reserved. They do not as readily speak up and aggressively state what is on their minds. Sometimes you have to read between the lines and try to figure out what their feelings are. Islanders are not likely to tell you, "We want you to do *this,* but not *that.*" They might say, "There is this kind of situation," and then subtly indicate what they want you to address.

People of Asian backgrounds and Pacific Island backgrounds share a certain indirectness and subtlety of communication that is a matter of politeness and courtesy. One reason Americans need to become more sensitive to this is simply to keep more accurate track of what positions are actually being taken. Americans need to work at this consciously, because there is a strong and often unconscious tendency for people from highly developed societies to believe that they know everything, that they are better than others, and that they can superimpose their values and ways of doing things on others. When people come from technologically and economically less developed cultures, there is an awful tendency for them to be stereotyped as not only doing things on a more modest scale but of being inferior.

PART OF MY CONCERN WITH THE AMERICAN FLAG GOVERNORS was the message their attitude was sending to other Pacific Islanders. If islanders under American rule were unhappy, it followed that the United States was not a reliable friend of independent Pacific nations. During the 1970s and 1980s, many of these new countries were formed from old colonial situations, and the leaders of the new countries began to find their voices. While Hawaii was integrally a part of the American system, I saw opportunities for Hawaii to play a special role in this new Pacific. I felt if we wanted the Pacific nations to be *our* friends, we had to be *their* friends, because genuine friendship does not merely come from giving speeches, but from taking action on specific concerns.

As a result of America's victory in World War II, we had become the great, unchallenged naval power of the Pacific, but during most of that time Americans were preoccupied with the containment of communism, the Cold War, and the armed conflicts in Korea and Vietnam. In point of fact, Americans began listening more carefully to the new Pacific nations after the tiny Republic of Kiribati[26] signed a fishing agreement with what then was called the Union of Soviet Socialist Republics (USSR). The USSR's interest in Kiribati, which now seems so obscure and inconsequential, drew the attention of powerful people in the U.S. government. From my contacts with the U.S. Navy's Pacific headquarters at Pearl Harbor, I knew that the presence of Russian intelligence-gathering ships was regarded with a deep sense of alarm. After becoming acquainted with Ieremia Tabai, president of the Republic of Kiribati, I asked him about the fishing rights agreement. He told me it had nothing to do with ideology. "It is strictly an economic deal in which the Russians are paying us," he said. "Otherwise nobody is willing to pay us for our fishing resources."

The United States did spend money in the Pacific, but it often did so without really consulting Pacific leaders. Like the American Flag governors, the Pacific Island leadership tended to feel that Americans were

---

[26] Pronounced *kir-i-bosh*

not particularly interested in them. Perhaps the most notable leader of the new Pacific nations was Sir Ratu Mara Kamisese, the prime minister of Fiji, who became my friend. To get the real needs of Pacific Islanders in better focus, a vehicle for dialogue and two-way participation with islanders was formed through the East-West Center. It was called the Pacific Island Development Program and consisted of twenty-three island governments scattered over the great expanses of Polynesia (which includes Hawaii), Micronesia, and Melanesia. By this time most of these were independent nations, such as Papua New Guinea, Vanuatu, and Western Samoa.

Through the Pacific Island Development Program, I came to see more clearly that America had to be concerned with the economic well-being of Pacific Islanders while respecting their different lifestyles. I began to focus on the idea of developing new technologies, or adapting existing technologies, that were appropriate to the needs of Pacific Islanders.

At first this evoked images in their minds of big, inappropriate foreign aid projects. They said, "We don't want technology. It will overwhelm us."

I said, "You have to think about the possibilities of small-scale technologies—appropriate technologies—that you can adapt to island environments."

Numerous meetings were held throughout the Pacific, with people from Hawaii playing catalytic roles.[27] The idea for an appropriate-technology agency became known as the Pacific International Center for High Technology Research, or PICHTR. There was interest in such an organization from within the U.S. government but money was tight, and I decided I needed to leverage the U.S. support.

I spoke with the foreign minister of Japan, Shintaro Abe. I was aware of Japan's interest in the Pacific community, and how important it was for everyone in the Pacific to work together. I told him the concept of a Pacific community unfortunately tended to be mostly talk. Nothing would really happen unless projects were undertaken to demonstrate concern. I told him Hawaii was in an ideal position to be a center for technology adaptation. I said I could help because I had extensive ties

[27]Particular credit should be given to Dr. Fujio Matsuda, then president of the University of Hawaii; Hideto Kono, director of the Department of Planning and Economic Development; Mufi Hanneman, then of my staff, now a City councilman; and Doris Ching, then of the College of Education, University of Hawaii. In Washington, the late U.S. Sen. Spark M. Matsunaga played an important role.

with the island leaders. "I can communicate with them, because they trust me," I said. "They feel comfortable with me. They say things to me they would never say to you or to American political leaders."

Hawaii, I said, could provide a knowledge-intensive service in technology while bringing the two great economic powers—Japan and America—together from both sides of the Pacific. The Japanese foreign minister liked my idea. "Please pursue it," he said. He said he would talk with Prime Minister Yasuhiro Nakasone, and that I likewise should talk with Prime Minister Nakasone. I did, and the prime minister told me I had a good idea that he would be happy to support.

I had people working with members of the staff of the Reagan Administration on the concept of PICHTR. Our understanding was that President Reagan would bring up PICHTR during his first Summit meeting with Nakasone in Tokyo, but somehow the subject was not discussed. I happened to be in Japan on the first Saturday after the Summit was over, and I met with Mr. Abe. He said that since PICHTR was an American-sponsored project he had not been free to bring it up. It had to originate from the American side. I said that was too bad, and I continued my effort.

The next time the president was going to Tokyo, I asked for a personal meeting. This time I wanted all the right staff to be present, meaning not only the president's staff but staff from U.S. military headquarters. We met at Hickam Air Field as President Reagan was passing through. I told the president that I had already talked with the Japanese, and that the Pacific Island leaders liked the idea. "It will not be just talking," I said, "but doing something concrete to show the United States and Japan working together to help Pacific Island nations." I stressed to the president that PICHTR would revolve around creating choices and options for the Pacific Islanders, and not forcing solutions on them. Would he please bring the matter up with Prime Minister Nakasone? Shortly thereafter U.S. Ambassador Mike Mansfield called me. He said the project was one of the first discussed. On the spot, Prime Minister Nakasone had said, "Wonderful. We will provide funding."

The last meeting I had with all the Pacific Islanders was in the Cook Islands, near the end of my last term in office. The heads of state of the Pacific Island Development Council went around the room thanking me for the role that Hawaii had played. They said, "As governor of Hawaii, you didn't need to do anything for us. But you thought about us, and we thank you."

They said they wanted to get moving right away. That was in late

1985. I immediately had PICHTR organized as a non-profit corporation, and shortly after I left office PICHTR got its first million-dollar
check. Japanese funding at the rate of a million dollars a year continues
to this day.

PICHTR works on a variety of technologies. The most exciting is
our effort to design an appropriately sized Ocean Thermal Energy
Conversion (OTEC) plant. Our goal is to complete all of the design
work for construction of an OTEC plant in one of the island nations of
the Pacific. The present plan is for it to be totally funded by Japan.

MY RELATIONSHIP WITH FOREIGN MINISTER Shintaro Abe was an example of the type of friendship we in Hawaii need if we are to realize our
potential in the Pacific. I first got to know Mr. Abe in Honolulu, and he
asked me to call him whenever I went to Tokyo. Subsequently he invited
me to his son's wedding. He also invited me to the eighty-eighth birthday party of his father-in-law, Nobusuke Kishi, who had been prime
minister right after the war. There were about five thousand people at
Kishi's party, but other than myself all the people who were asked to
speak were heads of state or their representatives.

I told Ambassador Mansfield, "I feel embarrassed, because you represent the country, and everybody else is speaking for their country."

He told me, "Don't feel like that. Friendship is important too."

When Shintaro Abe was ill during the last year of his life, I was one
of the few people who got to see him. I called his son when I was in
Tokyo and asked how his father was doing. Mr. Abe came on the telephone and insisted on knowing where I was, and that I come over.

ON TWO OCCASIONS WHILE I WAS GOVERNOR, President Carter recognized the unique role of Hawaii in national affairs by asking me to represent the United States in diplomatic roles. I headed the U.S. delegation
to the independence ceremony of the Republic of Kiribati. I also accompanied President Carter to Japan for the funeral of Prime Minister
Masayoshi Ohira. After the heads of state were seated, our delegation
was escorted in. It consisted of the president, Secretary of State Edmund
Muskie, Ambassador Mansfield, and myself. Our seats were in the center
in front. There were dozens of cameras shooting away as we sat down,
and then the memorial service began.

The fact that I was the first American governor of Asian ancestry created a certain level of interest that helped initiate international relationships. But my keen personal interest in these people was an indispens-

able part of actually developing these relationships. Han Xu was my first friend from Mainland China, or what the press at the time called Red China. Before the United States recognized the People's Republic of China and resumed normal relations, the Republic brought a valuable art exhibit to Hawaii under the sponsorship of the East-West Center. Jean attended the exhibition and invited Han Xu to have lunch with us at Washington Place. The enmity with China then was such that Han Xu was delighted that she had asked him to come. We developed a close friendship. Han Xu went on to become the head of China's liaison office with America. After full diplomatic relations were established, he became the Chinese ambassador to the United States. When I was in Washington, I would be invited to the liaison office and then the Chinese embassy. The other governors asked me how I got invitations for lunch when they did not, which to me was an interesting example of Hawaii's special relationship with the Pacific Rim.

After I was no longer governor, when Han Xu was meeting with the Commander-in-Chief of the Pacific (CINCPAC) people, he would tell them to please invite Jean and me to the receptions. He would give me a big embrace, which is a rare thing for Asians, but I had that kind of relationship with him.

I experienced many times in which a person of modest rank ascended to a position of great influence. When I met the current head of Taiwan's judicial system, he was a governor. He asked me if I spoke a little Japanese.

"*Sukoshi*," I said.

"*Nihongo de hanashimasho ka?* (Can we speak in Japanese?)," he asked. Over time we became good friends.

I also became friends with a man who was mayor of the city of Taipei. Today he is president of Taiwan, and I still see him when I go there.

The identity of Hawaii, and the setting of Hawaii, provide an ideal basis for getting acquainted internationally. I began a friendly acquaintance with Prime Minister Tinsulanonda Prim of Thailand at a dinner at Washington Place. When I went to Thailand, the prime minister was seated on a chair in a big room. He rose and greeted me enthusiastically, saying that it was not how long people are acquainted but the quality of the relationship that matters. Whenever I've been in Thailand he has received me warmly. On one of his return trips, I arranged for him to speak at the East-West Center.

My most publicized relationship in the Pacific was with Ferdinand Marcos, president of the Philippines. When I met Marcos he appeared to be leading his country out of disarray into a more productive, secure future. He and his wife hosted me and Jean in Manila, and they in turn came to Washington Place. When Marcos imposed martial law in the Philippines I was concerned, but I accepted his explanation that it would be temporary. I also felt that we in the United States must deal with leaders of the Pacific as we found them. We cannot expect to recreate our own ideal conditions and have everyone fit into our mold.

Finally Marcos was pushed out of office by the People Power movement. As protesters filled the streets of Manila, the final blow was the U.S. government's intervention, in which he was airlifted out of Manila all the way to Honolulu. While the turmoil was building in the Philippines, I was attending a National Governors' Association meeting in Washington. I was informed that Marcos and his family were being transported to Hawaii, and that it might be appropriate for me to be in Hawaii when they came. I could not allow an old friend to arrive without being received by anyone. As I had done in better times, I greeted him at Hickam Air Base as he deplaned.

I was severely criticized by various people for my relationship with Marcos, and for my gesture of friendship when he fell. I am not indifferent to these criticisms, but I accept them in the broader context of my effort to build relationships for Hawaii throughout the Pacific.

Jean was very much a part of developing relationships for Hawaii on an international level. The most basic reason is her personal warmth. She is the kind of person you can meet and soon feel you have known for a long time. She helped inspire my belief that, while being knowledgeable of proper form, we must be ourselves.

That idea was put to the test almost immediately after the 1974 election, when we first moved into Washington Place. Practically our first and certainly our most famous visitors were Queen Elizabeth and her husband Prince Phillip. We organized a small dinner party in their honor. In preparation the protocol officers gave us advice in a steady stream. They particularly focused on our children, who were told, "You mustn't say anything unless a subject is brought up by the queen," and other such things, which in my mind create unnatural barriers between people. After the protocol officers left we gathered our children up and said, "It's important to be polite, but be yourselves. Our guests are parents and understand what it is to have children." On the night of the dinner Queen Elizabeth talked with the children about school, swimming, and recreation, and it was as pleasant as we told the children it would be.

Not long thereafter Emperor Hirohito and his wife visited Hawaii.

My favorite photograph from that much-photographed event was my mother graciously bowing to the emperor. It reflects the special feeling of the first-generation immigrants for the emperor of Japan. For one of the emperor's public appearances, I had a section of seats set aside for people 85 and older. Their arrival time was to be around six p.m., but at three o'clock I was notified that many were already seated—and in the hot sun of mid-afternoon. I sent a message that those seats were reserved for them, and to please get out of the sun, but they continued to sit and wait. When our party arrived, I suggested that the emperor greet them. This entailed a walk of about fifty yards. As the day had gone on, the State Department representative had become increasingly officious, and he flatly said no, the emperor would not greet these people who had waited so long. I leaned over to the State Department man and said, "This is Hawaii, and I am taking charge now." As the emperor approached the group, every head went into a deep bow. I saw tears coming down many of the people's checks, and I am sure the emperor saw this too.

As a result of such experiences with protocol officers, we came to realize they could be as fallible as any other category of human beings. When the King of Tonga was coming to dinner, the State Department told us he loved Hawaiian food but didn't drink alcohol or coffee. When we greeted him and his wife on arrival, Jean found out from the queen that the king actually loved Japanese food, and she quickly changed the menu. In a later visit we learned that he liked to have a glass of wine with his meal, and that he enjoyed coffee as well.

At a dinner gathering of governors on the Mainland, we got our first look at China's renowned Deng Xiaoping. In his remarks he playfully alluded to the industrious work of the protocol officers who knew of his appetite for veal, which was our dinner entrée. "I not only had veal for dinner but veal for lunch. Yesterday I also had veal for dinner and veal for lunch. I didn't know Americans were so fond of veal."

Being oneself results in taking delight in others regardless of rank. This can have surprising results. Once Jean struck up a conversation with a woman from Malaysia. This conversation evolved into a pleasant acquaintance. Subsequently this woman became queen of Malaysia, and she and her husband the king went out of their way to host a lunch for an entourage including me and Jean and a group of about thirty who were promoting travel to Hawaii. One of the ladies from Hawaii was curious about our relationship with the royal family, and the queen replied, "Mrs. Ariyoshi befriended me at a time when the king was not even in the line of succession. Had she befriended me later, I might not have been so impressed, but because I then was a 'nobody,' so to speak, I shall never forget Mrs. Ariyoshi's friendship."

Jean brought favorable attention to Hawaii by knowing protocol but not coming to rest on it. On one of our trips to Japan, which was hosted by the prefecture governors, my Japanese counterparts and I were to have an audience with the emperor. It was announced that spouses would not attend, but then the emperor found out that Mrs. Ariyoshi was with me. Suddenly it was announced that the wives would attend, and the wives all told Jean, "We're getting to meet the emperor, thanks to you."

Another time, right after normalization of our diplomatic relationship with China, the American National Governors Association organized a trip—again, it was announced, without spouses. Jean and I had lunch at China's liaison office in Washington, and the subject of the trip came up. Jean asked if it was true that wives were excluded. The Chinese replied that the decision regarding spouses was not theirs, but ours, meaning the Americans, and that wives would be welcomed. Jean went back to the director of the National Governors Association and told him about the conversation. She asked if he had intended to limit the trip to governors. He was surprised we had that kind of contact with the Chinese and said, "Absolutely not—we would like for wives to go." She suggested there had been a lapse in communication, and she asked if he would like her to reconfirm the Chinese viewpoint. The wives enjoyed the trip immensely and gave Jean the credit.

MY INTERNATIONAL EXPERIENCES AS GOVERNOR of Hawaii gave me a strengthened conviction about the possibilities of the East-West role Hawaii can play, but it won't just happen. We have to work at it constantly. We have to learn about the world while maintaining the confidence that comes from being ourselves.

Already we are an international center of education and training, quality health care and scientific research, yet in all these areas we have just begun to realize our potential. We are an international travel destination, attracting a wide range of nationalities, yet we have just begun to realize our potential in languages, multilingual publication, software development, and media production. We do some business in the Pacific, but we could do a lot of business in the Pacific.

Somewhere before us, there is a defining next step that has to do with more consciously embracing internationalization and thinking globally. This next step will synthesize our varied challenges into a single, sweeping challenge, in that it will require us to adjust in such diverse areas as education, economic development, the conduct of government, and even culturally. Taking this step will allow us to realize the next level of our potential in the Pacific, which is so demonstrably becoming the economic focal point of the future.

Far from being a cause for anxiety, internationalization will be not only financially rewarding but psychologically gratifying. It will bring together the best of our cultural traditions. It will focus our work in the present, and it will lead us to our future.

In the process, we will gain a greater appreciation of the native culture of Hawaii and what is called "local" culture, or multiculturalism, because these are our truly distinguishing cultural traditions. We are different. The spirit of aloha is real. If I had not known this from childhood, I would have learned it from visitors who had been touched by the kindness and courtesy of Hawaii's people.

People who come here, wanting to tell someone how much they enjoyed their journey, often end up writing to the governor of Hawaii. They often talk about the beauty of our Islands, but the writers are almost invariably prompted by someone in Hawaii who demonstrated the aloha spirit. One person told about stopping someone in Waikiki for directions. The Hawaii person explained carefully but when the visitor still seemed uncertain, he said, "Wait here. I have some business at the bank but it won't take long." He came out of the bank and gave the visitor a ride. The letters I received were modest but frequent examples of good will at work among people of widely varied backgrounds.

In the process of developing this tolerant, nurturing community, we have led the way in expanding the American dream. Thinking of "us" and "them" has been revealed as small and self-defeating. When people think of Hawaii, they think of widely varied people getting along, mingling and mixing. People from around the world are comfortable here. Most people who live here, and many people who visit here, have thrown off the constraints of racism and expanded their vision and inherent potential as human beings. In a world freed from the chains of prejudice, all are set free to flourish.

CHAPTER FOURTEEN

Our Next Step

ON MY LAST NIGHT AS GOVERNOR OF HAWAII, I had an extraordinary experience. I had tried to do everything I could to make a smooth transition and not leave problems for my successor. I worked hard up until the end, with no letting up. Most of my materials had been packed away for me, but on this last night I was at my desk in Washington Place, going through the things on my desktop.

I thought again of my father, Ryozo Ariyoshi. I again felt a sadness that he had not lived to experience the years while I was governor, but the thoughts he had given me had been so much with me, and had influenced so many of my decisions.

I thought of Governor Burns—particularly how unusual it was he had picked me out to have this experience even though I had not been part of his group. I felt I had brought about changes that Burns himself would have made if he had continued, even if some of his supporters within the Democratic Party would not agree. I hoped I had done him justice. I hoped he understood I wasn't a perfect person, but that I had done what I had to do.

I felt good about the future. Leadership is leading when you can, while you're there. It also is leaving behind young people who are ready to make their own decisions. I felt all the long conversations I had engaged in with young people were time well spent. I felt particularly that I had helped develop people's thinking about working toward a preferred future.

As I worked my way through my desktop, everything I picked up seemed to have some special meaning, or a little story. Suddenly I felt drained in a way that I never had felt in my life. I felt that everything had been sapped out of me. Deep inside, I felt I had given it everything I had.

Ritually, politicians say they are proud to have enjoyed the public's support. I will say it again when it is no longer obligatory: I was proud to be elected in such an extraordinary democratic process as Hawaii's, and I was proud to serve. I have an overwhelmingly positive feeling about everything that happened after 1954, about everything I did with Jack Burns, and about my more than thirteen years as governor.

DURING MY LAST YEAR IN OFFICE, 1986, the vitality of the Democratic Party again was up for critical examination. A few old-timers still claimed I had wrecked the party with my ideas of openness. Others said I had a methodical style that caused people to lose interest. Yet, spontaneously, a statewide process of political renewal sprang up within the Democratic Party called Hawaii Democratic Action. It resulted in dozens of grassroots sessions to elicit member's views on issues. It was led by a combination of old-timers and newcomers from the ranks of the party.

In the gubernatorial campaign that followed, Congressman Cec Heftel jumped off to a large lead over John Waihee. Cec Heftel had made a lot of money in broadcasting, and he had gone from there to spending a large sum of money on winning a congressional seat. Waihee had been a young leader of the Constitutional Convention of 1978, which produced the native Hawaiian amendments. In 1980, John was elected to the House of Representatives and then, after only one two-year term, he ran successfully for lieutenant governor in 1982. John was a loyal lieutenant governor. He wanted to work with me. He asked for assignments where he thought he could be helpful, and I gave them to him. I asked him to help me with the United Airlines strike, and he went to Washington to find ways to ease the strike's burden on Hawaii. He got involved with agriculture issues and workmen's compensation. When I felt I needed help, I turned to him. He asked for direct access to the cabinet and to information within the Administration. I said, "Be my guest." He did these things in a nice way, and I trusted him. He played his role with obvious interest and intelligence. He understood that only one person can be governor at a time. As we worked, I could remember myself when I was lieutenant governor, and I could remember the many ways Governor Burns had helped me build an understanding of the government.

It is obvious from my story, and from what is known about history, that Governor Burns was preoccupied with the question of who would succeed him. Like Governor Burns, I shared a concern that the government not fall into the hands of a destructive type of person, but I was not preoccupied with the issue of succession to the extent Burns had been. With that as preface, I should add that early in my last term of office John Waihee expressed his interest in running for governor. He asked for my support, and I told him I thought he would make a good governor.

As the campaign approached, I made a more explicit decision. I had never known Cec Heftel well, but I did not have a strong sense of his commitment to Hawaii's people—not that it wasn't there, but I didn't feel it or experience it. I did not sense he truly understood Hawaii. I accordingly made it clear to John that I would support him, but in my own way, and in my own time frame.

I stressed to John that he must put together his own group, program, and identity. If he was to overcome Heftel's big lead and enormous financial resources, he had to go out and win it for himself. The polls said his task was almost impossible. He made some visible progress but it appeared it was not nearly enough.

Nonetheless I believed John could win, because I saw he had an ever-growing core of people who were willing to work hard. John reflected an intense desire to serve Hawaii, coupled with an expanding knowledge of State government and many ideas about how to achieve his goals. His program, priorities, and sense of timing were different from mine, but I had good feelings about him, and the point came when I gave him all the help I could. I think I played a significant role in pulling people behind him, adding to an excellent grassroots campaign. John had highly committed support, whereas Heftel had the softer support in which a person may say they are going to vote for someone but aren't ready to go out and work. When you interpret survey research, you have to keep that question in mind. Who has the most enthusiastic and committed core supporters? On primary election day, John pulled off a big upset victory. He went on to defeat Andy Anderson in the general election.

For more than six years his governorship was met with acclaim, and much of the balance of his governorship was met with considerable criticism. By 1994, most people thought the era of Democratic governors surely was over, but Ben Cayetano came from far behind to beat the Republican Patricia Saiki and Frank Fasi, who ran as an independent. The victory of Ben Cayetano and the Democratic Party occurred in spite of a Republican tide that swept the rest of the country, in which Congress fell to the control of the Republican Party for the first time in forty years. As a result, the Democratic Party now has won the governorship of Hawaii for thirty-six straight years, starting with Burns' election in 1962 and moving through nine successful campaigns, at four years per term.

Throughout this time, the Republican Party failed to revive. Its base in the State Legislature actually got smaller. It went from being a small political party to a minuscule one. What was left of Republican talent was poured into trying to win the governorship, which I think the Republicans viewed as a sort of instant restoration of their base of power. The Republicans made the mistake of believing that political control comes from the top. That was why they were fixated on the gover-

norship. Like Frank Fasi, they talked about The Machine as if they really believed in its existence. But the very idea of a political machine is of
the political strongman and the smoke-filled room. It is the idea of a succession of corrupt, autocratic figures who operate in a closed system.

I was governor longer than anyone, and obviously I was not the
"boss" type. On the contrary, all of my instincts had to do with creating
an open system and helping others participate fully and effectively. In
fact, at times I myself had behaved as a political maverick as a result of
following my beliefs rather than following the party's platform.

However, what was true then, and is still true today, is that we had a
vast and highly effective campaign organization of committed, believing
people. I had my own network of hundreds and then thousands of supporters, built up over many campaigns, many serious discussions, and
many difficult judgment calls. This was true for others within the Democratic Party as well. By and large, not only the winners but those who
lost elections in the Democratic primary clung to the name and the standards of the Democratic Party. Other than Fasi, people who lost did not
bolt the party. Rather, they poured their concerns, thoughts, and feelings
back into the party and gave it new energy. People of all factions formed
relationships at the grassroots level that endure despite the shifting fortunes of politics.

This process of building a large, vibrant political party went on and on,
not over years but decades. For my part, even after I was governor I sometimes had as many as five or six events to attend each day during a campaign. I sometimes would spend just as long at a coffee hour as I had when
I was a legislator. The conversation would start, and the concerns would
begin to flow, and the bonds of relationship would be formed. People left
saying they not only would vote but go out and work, and they did.

In a healthy political system, control comes from the bottom up.
This foundation needs to be built in the smallest elected district, which is
the House of Representatives. It is the best base for gaining control of
the top offices. District representatives are out in the community. They
make so much direct contact. They shape and mold public opinion, sell
policies to the voters, and give feedback if people are unhappy.

If you look back to 1954, our Democratic Party effort went into con-
trolling the Territorial House, and we got the Senate in the process.
When we lost the Congressional Delegate's race in 1954, we came back
and won it in 1956 and 1958 based on our strength in the Territorial
House. A similar thing was true in the State elections of 1962. We got
Burns in as governor as a result of our grassroots strength in the House.

The Republican Party, by not building a grassroots base, was doomed to chronic failure. Its fixation on totally changing its fortunes by winning the governorship reflected a kind of elitism, and for forty years it has not succeeded. I should add that the overwhelming electoral success of the Democratic Party is not a totally unmixed blessing, because Hawaii is virtually a one-party state as a result. This puts a special burden on the Democratic Party to scrutinize itself and bring forth good programs, good policies, and good people. We cannot delude ourselves that things are going all that well. We cannot be negative, and divided, and expect our society to continue enjoying the good life.

I FEEL VERY STRONGLY THAT WE MUST PUT ASIDE the current sense of gloom. To get back on a positive track, we need to remind ourselves of who and what we are. We need to return to the practices of mutual obligation, respect for one another, and cooperation, to the concept of *otagai,* in the words of my father, or the aloha spirit, in the vocabulary of the native culture of Hawaii.

As a unique island state, we must not follow the national pattern of self-defeating pessimism. Rather, we must relocate our sense of destiny for Hawaii. Good leadership, and good citizenship, are crucial.

We must re-ignite our sense of fair play. We have a shared future and a shared fate.

We must re-ignite our intense determination to live by the principles of equality and opportunity. Earlier I suggested that some of the companies coming into Hawaii have old-fashioned, condescending attitudes. They must be engaged in a learning process. How are they to change if we do not aggressively help them change? To do this, we must be honest and constantly take stock.

We must manage finances carefully, holding the line in good times so that in difficult times we can continue to be compassionate. If sacrifices are to be made, all should join in making them, with an understanding of why we are sacrificing and where we are going. When times are difficult, we should continue to generate new ideas and new ways of doing things.

We must take care of not only the crises, but bear in mind that accomplishment is built on doing little things right, over and over. To really achieve our goals necessitates that many people be involved in the art of governing, and that each person do his or her best.

The zeal for good planning needs to be revived. We are making positive strides in environmental management, but we cannot relax. On the contrary, we should push our thinking to the next level, and think about all our resources in terms of long-term sustainability and long-term carrying capacity. We should tailor our activities to those long-term standards. Further, we should not divorce economic development from planning, but recognize that economic activity generates immediate impacts on the areas that require care in planning.

It is time for us to again ask what we want Hawaii to be. What kind of economy do we want? What kind of jobs? What should the pattern of land use be? How much growth can we realistically sustain?

In our public discussions, we would benefit from lowering our voices and having more real conversation with one another. A sense of direction cannot be generated from public relations, but rather from genuine dialogue. Political vision is not something that can be run up like a flag at campaign time. The word "vision" is apt for ideas that are deeply held, discussed over and over, and worked at for as long as it takes to accomplish them.

Collectively we have to become better informed. We have to look more deeply into questions that may seem uninteresting, or frustrating. But when we realize that what we do in such areas as education, economic development, and government finance will determine the quality of our lives, and the lives of future generations, we will have a much better understanding of these issues.

We must return to the long view. We must overcome what seems to be a current sense of myopia. We have obligations to the future by which we will ultimately be judged. By taking the long view, by getting back in touch with a sense of destiny, we will approach the future confidently and with a sense of excitement, because the future of Hawaii is potentially very bright.

Across the years, I personally have retained an inner feeling of excitement which, thankfully, has never deserted me. I think I inherited Papa's energy and Mother's perpetual optimism. I was supported by my wife and children, and motivated by them. If they had not supported me, I could not have served, but they made it easy for me. I experienced my time in office without letdown or fatigue, without burnout or despair.

I had that one extraordinary moment, alone at my desk, in my last night as governor, when I felt so totally drained. After a night's sleep, I was up and running again. To have joined with thousands of other people in transforming Hawaii from a politically backward territory to a progressive, multiracial state, has been rewarding beyond imagination. I do believe this most essential accomplishment of the Democratic Party is a beacon that lights up American democracy and can be seen around the world.

But our obligation to the future compels us to not rest on past accomplishments. We have new challenges to meet, and we must get on with the process. *Otagai.* We are obligated to one another. *Okage sama de.* We are what we are because of one another. To see things whole, to go for the long term, to act as stewards—these are the things that are most important, when all is said and done.

EPILOGUE

AT MY LAST PRESS CONFERENCE AS GOVERNOR, I was asked two questions. First, would I ever consider a lucrative position on the board of trustees of Bishop Estate? Absolutely not, I said, because I think it is inappropriate for a former governor to use his accumulated contacts in such a way.

Would I golf? I said I would golf a lot, but truthfully I haven't golfed nearly as much as I wanted. People often ask, "What do you do since you retired?" I say that I merely changed jobs. When I finished my last year in office, I was 59. I became active in a variety of businesses that revolve around quality and innovation.

In my public service roles, I follow the principle that positive people are the most effective. I am a staunch supporter of Nature Conservancy, for example, because I feel its members are positive and get real work done. I have helped them make contacts in Asia, expanding their organization and spreading the conservation ethic. I tend to serve on boards of organizations that have vital meaning to Hawaii but also reach out beyond Hawaii. I still serve on the board of the Pacific International Center for High Technology Research, which continues its work and still receives funding from Japan. I am chairman of the board of governors of the East-West Center, and serve on the boards of the Queen's (Medical Center) International Corporation, Bishop Museum, and the Japan-America Institute of Management Science.

I was appointed by President Clinton to serve on the Advisory Committee for Trade Policy and Negotiations. It is made up mostly of the chief executives of large American corporations, such as Chrysler, Proctor and Gamble, AT & T, etc. I am one of the few members who do not represent special interest groups, and my background in Hawaii and the Pacific often leads me to weigh in with opinions that challenge the thinking of the corporations.

I am president and founding member of the Center for International Commercial Dispute Resolution, a member of the Japan-Hawaii Economic Council, and honorary co-chair of the Japanese American National Museum. I am the American advisor to the U.S.-Japan space program. I serve on the advisory board of the Japan Foundation Center for Global Partnership. I am one of several American advisors who assist in establishing guidelines for funding. The Shintaro Abe fund, in memory of the foreign minister of Japan, is part of the Center's program.

Finally, I maintain my commitment to the Democratic Party as Democratic National Committeeman, over forty years after my friend Tom Ebesu invited me to the meeting, and my mentor Jack Burns said, "You should run for office." If you recall, I turned to see if there was someone behind me but no, he was talking to me.

INDEX

Abe, Shintaro, 187, 189, 204
Abercrombie, Neil, 154
agriculture, diversification of, 107-110
aquaculture, 124
Akihito, Crown Prince (of Japan), 181, 182, 183
Akita, George, 13
Alaska, 47
alternate energy sources, 122-125
Americans of Japanese Ancestry (AJAs), 14, 32, 33-34, 35, 87, 115
Anderson, Andy, 140, 197
Anderson, Eileen, 146
Ariyoshi, Donn (son), 18, 75
Ariyoshi, George: board member of First Hawaiian Bank, 171-173; chairman of Senate Public Utilities Committee, 58-60; chairman of Senate Ways and Means Committee, 50-54; childhood, 20-21, 30-33; critics of, 113-114, 125-126; and family time, 135-137; and father's death, 81-82; governing philosophy of, 22-23, 89-95; as governor, 85-86, 141; as lieutenant governor, 73-80, 83-84; and marriage, 44; and law practice, 35-36, 56, 74, 145; and post-gubernatorial activities, 183, 203-204; Senate Majority Floor Leader, 60. See also elections
Ariyoshi, Jean (wife), 17, 36, 44, 156, 183; and knowledge of protocol, 191, 192-193; and preservation of Washington Place, 163-165
Ariyoshi, Lynn, (daughter), 18, 75
Ariyoshi, Mitsue (mother), 18, 21, 32, 40, 183; illness and death of, 154-156
Ariyoshi, Ryozo (father), 18, 20, 29-30, 35, 183, 195; death of, 81-82; personal beliefs of, 21-22, 31, 60; as campaign worker, 40, 47

Ariyoshi, Ryozo (son), 18, 75
Ariyoshi, Sky (grandson) 157
astronomy center 121

Bellinger, Johnny, 172
Beppu, Tadao, 57
Bishop Estate, 58-59
Bitterman, Mary, 149, 150
Blaisdell, Neal S., 138
Brown, Kenneth F., 57, 73
Burns, John A.: early career, 70-72; as governor, 49, 50, 57, 76-77 83-84, 121, 152, 157, 170; illness and death, 83, 85, 86-88; legacy of, 18, 20, 79, 195; looking for a successor, 69, 73-75; meetings with 38-39, 54-55, 72, 78, 80; molder of the Democratic Party, 74, 78-80
Buyers, John "Doc," 109-110, 165

campaign financing system, 161-162
Cane Fires (Okihiro), 13
Carter, Jimmy, 122
Cary, Miles, 32
Cayetano, Ben, 165, 197
Ching, Doris, 187
Cleveland, Harlan, 157
Clinton, President Bill, 183
Coffman, Tom, 11-14
Constitutional Conventions, 84, 174, 196
Cravalho, Elmer, 46
Craven, John, 123
Crossley, Randolph, 52, 87, 140

DeLima, Frank, 139
DeMello, Eddie, 69
Democratic Party, 41, 48, 50, 80-81, 138-139, 152 factionalism in, 18, 46, 57, 72; and land reforms, 53, 59; molding of, 71-72, 74, 78-79; and

PRODUCTION NOTES

Composition, paging, and design were done
by Steve Shrader Graphic Design, Honolulu,
on a Macintosh Quadra 800 using QuarkXPress 3.3.
The typeface is Berthold Baskerville Book.

Offset presswork and binding were done
by The Maple-Vail Book Manufacturing Group.
Text paper is Glatfelter Offset Smooth Antique, basis 50.